DISCOVER CANADA

Northwest Territories

By Lyn Hancock

Consultants

Desmond Morton, FRSC, Professor of History, University of Toronto

Charles D. Arnold, Ph.D., Director, Prince of Wales Northern Heritage Centre, Yellowknife

Nolan Swartzentruber, Director, Dehcho Divisional Board of Education, Fort Simpson

 Grolier Limited
TORONTO

Cumberland Sound
Overleaf: **Wilberforce Canyon, Hood River**

Dedication: For my husband, Frank Schober

Canadian Cataloguing in Publication Data

Hancock, Lyn, 1938-
  Northwest Territories

(Discover Canada)
ISBN 0-7172-2722-7

1. Northwest Territories — Juvenile literature.
I. Title. II. Series : Discover Canada (Toronto, Ont.)

FC4161.2.H3 1993   971.9   C93-095016-7
F1090.5.H3 1993

Printed and bound in Canada.
Published simultaneously in the United States.
1 2 3 4 5 6 7 8 9 10   DWF   99 98 97 96 95 94 93

Front cover: Virginia Falls, Nahanni National Park Reserve
Back cover: Polar bear

"Rainbow Valley," the Dene village Ndilo, in Yellowknife's Old Town

Table of Contents

Chapter 1   Canada's Outback.....7
Chapter 2   The Land.....9
Chapter 3   The Environment.....19
Chapter 4   The People.....29
Chapter 5   Early Adventurers.....37
Chapter 6   Opening the North.....47
Chapter 7   The Growth of Communities.....55
Chapter 8   Government.....61
Chapter 9   Today's Economy.....69
Chapter 10 Culture and Recreation.....79
Chapter 11 Communication.....91
Chapter 12 Tourism: Within Reach, Yet Beyond Belief.....97
Facts at a Glance.....111
Maps.....123
Index.....126

CHAPTER ONE

Canada's Outback

Welcome to the Northwest Territories! We're that huge, pie-shaped chunk of Canada north of the rest of the country. We stretch from the sixtieth parallel all the way to the North Pole. Many people mix us up with Alaska or the Yukon, but we're neither. In fact, there's no place on Earth like the Northwest Territories.

Life is exciting here in the North. History is happening now, and it's happening fast. One day soon, the name Northwest Territories won't even be on the map because we're going to divide ourselves into two new territories.

The Northwest Territories, or NWT as it is commonly known, differs greatly from other parts of Canada — in its huge size, its amazing landscapes, its surprising climate, its contrasting peoples and its unique form of government. Did you know, for example, that more than half of the residents of the NWT are Native people? Even the NWT licence plate stands out with its blue and white polar bear. We northerners feel different, too. Perhaps that's why, when we travel down south, we say we're going "outside."

The NWT is largely unknown, and what people think they know about us is often plain wrong. Come with us now for a taste of what it's really like up here.

One thing visitors to the NWT *can* expect is the unexpected — like this patch of domestic flowers growing in the hollows of smooth Canadian Shield rock.

CHAPTER TWO

The Land

The land has special meaning for the aboriginal peoples of the NWT. They say the land is their life, their blood and their mother. The Inuit call it Nunassiaq, or "the beautiful land," and they call their homeland Nunavut, which means "our land." The Dene call their homeland Denendeh, "the land of the people."

Non-aboriginal people also have special feelings for the land. Some are drawn to the wide-open spaces, the silence and solitude, the pure air and water, the seemingly endless wilderness and the abundant and untamed wildlife. They enjoy a sense of freedom here, and a feeling of being where few have been before. Others come in pursuit of furbearing animals, whales, gold, oil or diamonds. They all relish the joy of discovery. The North is magnetic; there is a saying that once you drink of a northern river, you will return.

Size and Area

The vast NWT covers over 3 million square kilometres (1 million square miles) of land, or about a third of the total area of Canada. It stretches from the James Bay islands in the south to Ellesmere Island in the north, and spans four time zones from Baffin Island in the east to the Yukon in the west. Its coastline contains numerous bays, inlets and islands. Many areas have only recently been mapped and many have not yet been explored.

Bear Rock, a famous landmark at the junction of the Mackenzie and Bear rivers

The Landscapes

The NWT is an epic land of spectacular landscapes including the deep canyons of Nahanni National Park, the salt plains of Wood Buffalo National Park, and the awe-inspiring ice sheets of Ellesmere and Auyuittuq national parks. It is home to many great wilderness waterways, including four Canadian Heritage Rivers: the Nahanni, Thelon, Kazan and Soper. Its vast lakes are more like inland seas, and its distinctive waterfalls, such as Wilberforce and Virginia, would be as well known as Niagara if they were less remote. The NWT also holds unique landmarks such as the pingos, or ice-cored hills, of Tuktoyaktuk.

The Canadian Shield

Three-quarters of the NWT is covered by the Canadian, or Precambrian, Shield, an immense horseshoe of solid bedrock that is 2 to 4 billion years old. The Shield extends well beyond the NWT

Right: The turbulent Hood River carves its way through Precambrian rock to plunge 49 metres (160 feet) at Wilberforce Falls. These are the highest falls north of the Arctic Circle. *Far right:* Fresh snow and sea ice at Alexandra Fiord, Ellesmere Island

and is the storage place for a great deal of Canada's mineral wealth. Much of it is covered by layers of younger sedimentary rocks, forests and thick vegetation, so minerals are hard to reach. But on the treeless Arctic tundra, the bedrock lies on the surface for all to see.

In most of the NWT's Shield country, low rock and gravel hills are interspersed with patches of wet, spongy muskeg and millions of little low-lying lakes. But along the east coast of the islands from Baffin to Ellesmere, the land rises like the edge of a saucer to form a spine of high mountains and snowfields that plunge into deep fiords.

Mountains and Plains

In the west, the Mackenzie Mountains, along with the Richardson and Selwyn mountains, divide the NWT from the Yukon. The Mackenzie range is probably the most extensive uninhabited mountain range in the world. Only in the last 20 years have many of its unique landforms been explored.

Left: Polje, or giant sinkhole, in the Ram Plateau. Poljes quickly turn to grassy meadows after rain, but dry up just as readily. *Below:* Stalactite in Igloo Cave, one of hundreds of ice caves in the Ram Canyons

Within this range, the Nahanni River and Ram Plateau have the deepest and most complex river canyons in Canada, some say the world. Nearby are unusual limestone rock labyrinths, grassy meadows formed from giant sinkholes, terraced hot springs, and ancient ice caves littered with the skeletons of wild sheep.

Between the Mackenzie Mountains and the Canadian Shield lies the northernmost section of the Great Plains, which stretch northward all the way from the Gulf of Mexico. This prairie, or lowland, consists of sediments (dust, silt, rocks and other debris) deposited at the bottom of what was once an inland sea. It holds most reserves of oil and gas in the NWT.

Ice Sheets

The Earth has experienced many ice ages, in which ice plowed down from the Far North to cover the land. The last ice age began about 18 000 years ago. Immensely thick ice sheets moved southward, pushing in front of them great piles of rocks, sand and gravel, which gouged, carved and scraped the land bare. Then the ice gradually melted away, leaving behind vast piles of stones and pebbles, huge boulders, long sand and gravel ridges, and clumps of low, rounded hills. They also polished and sculpted the rocks.

Baffin Island mountains and glacier, seen from the air

Rocks! The story goes that God make the Earth and all the living things on it in five days; on the sixth day He made the Northwest Territories; and on the seventh day He sat back and threw rocks at it! That's just a joke, but it does indicate how rocky the landscapes are in the NWT.

And water! There's so much water in the NWT that, looking down from the air in summer, you wonder if you're seeing islands in the sea or lakes in the land. When the ice sheets melted, water filled the hollows and formed countless streams and lakes. Free of its heavy burden of ice, the land rose. As a result, you can now find shells and bones of marine mammals far inland and high above sea level.

Permanent ice caps, remnants of the great ice sheets that once covered all of Canada, still cover much of the eastern Arctic Islands. Two of the best known are the Barnes and Penny ice caps on Baffin Island.

Water

The NWT contains about 24 percent of Canada's fresh water and some of the Earth's few remaining unpolluted lakes and rivers. These are the breeding grounds for all manner of wildlife — including hordes of insects. Waterways also function as highways in this immense country, whether for boats in summer or sleds and snowmobiles in winter.

The most important waterway is the Slave-Mackenzie River system. It begins in the Rocky Mountains and surges northward over 3000 kilometres (2000 miles) of forests, valleys and tundra to empty into the Arctic Ocean. It drains about one-fifth of Canada, an area twice the size of Ontario. In fact, the Mackenzie is Canada's largest as well as its longest river system. In the world, only the Amazon and the Missouri-Mississippi systems are larger. The Dene name for the Mackenzie, Dehcho, means "big river."

For its last 240 kilometres (150 miles), the mighty Mackenzie seems to shatter into a million fragments. This is the Mackenzie River Delta,

The Mackenzie River Delta, near Inuvik. One of the largest deltas in the world, this vast maze of islands, ponds and streams is also one of the world's greatest wildlife habitats.

a vast jigsaw puzzle of muddy, brown channels, multicoloured lakes, islands, ponds, peatbogs and muskeg. People say that you could set someone down in the delta, turn him around twice, and he would be lost forever.

During the ice-free season between May and October, the Mackenzie River is navigable for its entire length. All summer, a whole variety of vessels ply the waters from Hay River, on Great Slave Lake, to and along the Arctic coastline, including pleasure boats, coastguard vessels and tugs pushing barges loaded with supplies for camps and settlements.

Wilder rivers drain the Barren Lands in central NWT. Adventurers come from around the world to canoe these wilderness waters. The most popular are the Coppermine, Hood, Burnside and Back rivers, all of which head for the Arctic Ocean; and the Thelon and Kazan rivers, which empty into Baker Lake and thus Hudson Bay.

Left: Lead, or narrow channel of open water, in the ice near Mt. Asgard, Baffin Island. *Above:* At anchor on the East Arm of Great Slave Lake

The two biggest lakes in the NWT are Great Bear Lake, the most northerly of the world's major lakes and the fourth largest in North America, and Great Slave Lake, the fifth largest in North America.

The largest body of water in the NWT is the Arctic Ocean, but most of its surface area is covered all year by a thick layer of sea ice called the polar ice pack. This ice looks as solid as land, but it isn't. It shifts back and forth at the whim of the wind, water currents and tides.

In places, this densely packed ice covers the entire surface of the water as if it were a huge snowy field, but in other places it breaks into moving pieces called floes or pans. Often the floes smash into each other, throwing blocks of ice high into the air. These are called pressure ridges. In still other places, the ice cracks apart to create a narrow pathway of water called a lead. Much larger openings between ice floes are called polynyas. These often appear in the same place year after year, providing breathing holes and landing or feeding stations for birds and mammals.

Land Ice and Permafrost

Icebergs float on the sea, but they are not made of sea ice. Instead, they form when huge pieces of glacier ice crack off and tumble into the sea. Above water, icebergs can loom as tall as some apartment buildings — and that's only a fraction of their total height. In fact, seven-eighths of an iceberg is hidden underwater. Most of the icebergs seen in the NWT come from Greenland or Ellesmere Island.

Almost anywhere in the NWT, if you dig a little way into the earth you will hit permafrost, or permanently frozen ground. Permafrost is made up of topsoil, rock and ice. Above the permafrost is a shallow layer of active soil, which freezes in winter but thaws in summer, thereby allowing plants to grow. A covering of snow and vegetation insulates the ground and protects the permafrost. This frozen ground keeps the rainwater and other surface water on the land for plants and animals to use during the short growing season. Otherwise the limited water supply would seep deep into the ground and be lost.

In summer, if you remove the soil's insulating cover of vegetation, the permafrost melts, the soil slumps, and anything on top sinks — including houses. That's why northerners build roads on gravel mounds (called berms) and houses on stilts or gravel pads, why we

Right: Because of the permafrost, houses in Inuvik sit above the ground on posts, and smaller pipes inside this utilidor carry heat and water into them and sewage out.
Far right: Building a house on top of a steel frame at Paulatuk — a new way to construct over permafrost.

transport hot water in elevated, insulated pipes (called utilidors) and support pipelines above ground.

Patterned Ground

When you look down on the tundra landscape in summer, especially from the air, you can see circles, stripes and other interesting patterns. These occur where water trapped in the thin layer of soil above permafrost freezes and thaws over and over again. Polygons (five-sided depressions) look like giant sunken honeycombs. Hummocks are small mounds of soil that look like mops and are very difficult to walk on. Pingos, pyramid-shaped hills with cores of ice inside, look like mini-volcanoes. Then there are frost boils, soil creeps, boulder streams and frost fractures.

In the brief summer, both the land and the sea make everchanging patterns. But in winter, which takes up most of the year, they look like one vast, white wasteland — and you can't tell where the land ends and the sea begins.

Far left: **Iceberg. The patterned ground of the tundra: polygons** (*left*) **and pingos** (*below*).

CHAPTER THREE

The Environment

Living in the Far North is unique in many ways. For one thing, the sun does not rise and set every day of the year as it does farther south.

On the map, the NWT is cut in half at 66½°N latitude by an imaginary line known as the Arctic Circle. North of this line the sun doesn't set for at least one summer day each year. As you continue north, you get more and more days in which the sun stays above the horizon all night long. In winter the opposite happens. North of the Arctic Circle, the sun doesn't rise for at least one day each year, and the farther you go, the more such days there are. At the North Pole, there are six months of constant light and six months of constant dark.

You can get a strange feeling, around Christmas time, if you see that your watch says, for example, ten o'clock, but there's nothing to tell you whether it's ten o'clock in the morning or ten o'clock at night. It all looks the same outside: dark. It feels just as strange in summertime to know it's midnight when the sun is still shining. That's why the land north of the Arctic Circle is called the Land of the Midnight Sun.

The Tree Line

Geographers divide the NWT into two natural regions, the Arctic and the Subarctic, with the tree line marking the division. Generally speaking, trees only grow south of the tree line, in the Subarctic, where the average temperature in July is at least 10°C (50°F).

The Mackenzie Delta at midnight in midsummer

The tree line is not a distinct and straight line stretching from west to east as you might expect. Rather, it is a wavy band of scrubby trees and bushes alternating with patches of tundra vegetation, such as lichens, mosses and flowering plants. This band snakes diagonally from the Mackenzie Delta in the northwest to near Churchill, Manitoba, in the southeast. In certain places, depending on local conditions, you may find pockets of trees well north of the tree line.

Climate

Many people think that the NWT is covered with snow and ice all year long, and that it's always cold, cold, cold. Well, they're wrong.

The NWT gets less snow than many places in southern Canada, and the snow that does fall often gets swept around by howling winds. It rarely rains. Most of the Arctic is so dry that scientists classify it as a desert. Temperatures have been known to fall to below -50 °C (-60 °F) in winter, but summers are surprisingly warm — sometimes even hot. In the Subarctic, July temperatures of 40 °C (104 °F) have been recorded in Fort Smith. And at times, people even go swimming in the Arctic Ocean.

For eight or nine months of the year, most of the NWT actually is as people imagine it — wind-swept, snow-covered, featureless. But summer days are long and warm, and northerners make the most of them, turning even the Arctic Ocean into a playground.

On average, winters are colder in the NWT than in southern Canada. And harsh winds can make it feel colder yet. But it's not the actual cold that makes the NWT the coldest place in Canada. It's the duration of that cold. In the Arctic, freezing temperatures can occur in every month, and on average only 40 to 60 days are free of frost. So winter in the Arctic lasts at least nine months.

When spring finally returns, people celebrate: it's carnival time. Snow and ice still cover the ground, and the thermometer still lingers below zero; but there's a new brightness to the light, the days are longer, it feels warmer than it is, and best of all, there are no bugs yet. Summer is short, but long hours of daylight enable plants to grow quickly. In the Subarctic, there can be up to 100 frost-free days.

The aurora borealis, or the northern lights, are glowing curtains of white, blue, green and red light that run and dance all over the night sky. Best seen in late winter, they are caused by solar winds of electrically charged particles that are attracted to the Earth's magnetic North Pole, located in the Arctic Islands. When these electrons from space collide with other particles, they generate a huge amount of electrical energy. The particles then become fluorescent and light up the sky with their dazzling displays.

Plants

Let's say you are driving north from British Columbia or Alberta as far as you can go. When the road runs out (near Yellowknife), you continue on to the top of the world by private plane. You'll be fascinated to see how the vegetation changes as you travel north.

At first, along the Slave, Liard and Mackenzie rivers, you travel through the taiga, or boreal coniferous forest. The main trees in the taiga are spruce, birch, jack pine, aspen, poplar, alder and tamarack. On the forest floor are soft mats of moss, lichen and berry plants and a variety of shrubs.

As you go farther north, the trees gradually dwindle in number as well as size, giving way to a transition zone of stunted trees mixed with tundra vegetation. This zone, known as the Subarctic Forest-Tundra or the Land of Little Sticks, is a water-logged land full of bogs and muskeg.

Below: Autumn trees reflected in the waters of Great Slave Lake.
Right: Even the grey rocks of the Arctic Islands blaze with colour for a few weeks every year.

Farther north again, the trees eventually disappear. You have reached the vast Arctic Tundra zone, where long winters, lack of fresh water and poor soil make it difficult for plants to grow. But grow they do, once summer finally arrives. Fast and furiously, the eager plants soon cover the thin layer of soil with an incredible tapestry. Even the rocks are patterned by multicoloured lichens.

In the Arctic, survival is the name of the game. Every plant has its own strategy. The arctic willow and the rhododendron spread themselves flat on the ground to be out of the wind. The yellow arctic poppy uses its petals to follow the sun, while purple saxifrage and dwarf fireweed produce large, brightly coloured flowers, which are warmer than white flowers. The woolly lousewort has dense, fuzzy hair, and the moss campion and mountain avens form a clump to raise the temperature around them.

Wild flowers carpet the shores of lakes and streams in summer.
Insets, left to right: The black fruit of the evergreen crowberry shrub are edible and sweet, but rather bland; yellow cinquefoil and bright pink moss campion are just two of the many, many wildflowers that enliven northern landscapes.

Wildlife

The NWT is one of the world's last great refuges where scientists and tourists can see and study wild animals in their original habitats. Wildlife is particularly important to the aboriginal people of the NWT. It means more than hunting and fishing for fur and food. Being "on the land" with wildlife is a cultural and spiritual experience.

Non-aboriginal people who live here or come up to visit enjoy wildlife, too. For many, seeing wild animals that may never have seen a human being before is very exciting, especially close up or in large numbers. Imagine a polar bear with two cubs looking through your window, or several thousand caribou swimming across a river.

The Subarctic still supports healthy numbers of moose, Dall's sheep, black and grizzly bears, wolves and caribou, as well as valuable furbearers such as marten, muskrat and beaver. Wood Bison National Park, which is shared with Alberta, holds the last free-roaming herds of wood bison, the northernmost colony of white pelicans in North America, and the only nesting site of wild whooping cranes in the world. About 200 bird species nest in the Subarctic. Pike, pickerel, whitefish and lake trout are plentiful, partly because there are 10 000 species of insects for them to feed on.

The Arctic is one of the few areas of the world with still-thriving numbers of seals, walrus, whales, polar bears, musk-oxen, wolves, peregrine falcons and gyrfalcons. It has dense concentrations of birds — 400 pairs of snow geese may nest on a square kilometre (1/3 square mile) of tundra, and 100 000 seabirds will all nest together on one island.

Few species live in the NWT all year because winter conditions are so harsh, but hundreds of species visit each summer to breed and feed. The North then becomes an immense nursery with abundant space, lots of food, countless waterholes and constant daylight. Every spring and summer, tens of thousands of barren ground caribou travel from the taiga to the tundra to calve, forage

Clockwise from far left: The endangered whooping crane is making a comeback in Wood Buffalo National Park; a ground squirrel makes itself at home in a length of the abandoned Canol Pipeline; walruses bask in the sun off Hall Beach; the large, shaggy musk-ox is found across the continental tundra and on several Arctic Islands.

and grow fat. Meanwhile, hundreds of thousands of birds arrive from all over North and South America to mate, nest and raise their young. Some migrate incredible distances. Arctic terns make a 35 000 kilometre (22 000-mile) round trip from the Antarctic. They come to feed on krill, a tiny crustacean that lives only in cold waters.

Conservation

The Arctic ecosystem, or community of plants and animals, is more fragile than other ecosystems in the world. At times, and in certain places, there seems an incredible abundance in the North. But the many animals belong to only a few species. This becomes a problem if one species goes down in numbers. For instance, if the krill were to disappear, the arctic tern would have nothing to eat. Furthermore some NWT species are unique in the world.

Arctic plants and animals are tough, but they live on the edge in more ways than one. Most species, for instance, lead a feast or famine existence at the whim of the weather. Snow geese may reach the tundra to find their nesting grounds buried in snowdrifts. Pods of narwhals or beluga whales that crowd together at familiar breathing holes may be trapped by incoming ice. Owls and foxes might find lemmings and snowshoe hares scurrying everywhere one year; the next, they may find just a few.

The Arctic ecosystem has always survived the difficulties thrown to it by nature. A much more serious threat comes as a result of human activity. In our pursuit of natural resources such as oil and gas, we tend to forget how much harm we can cause. One oil spill in the Arctic could devastate the whole ecosystem.

Industry is not the only threat. Individuals can damage the community too. Fish grow extremely slowly in cold northern waters. A ten-year-old lake trout weighs only 1 kilogram (2.2 pounds) in Great Bear Lake, but if it lived in Utah, it would have grown to about five times that size. If people take too many fish from a lake, it takes many decades for the fish to recover in numbers and size.

Guns, as well as the increasing numbers of roads and all-terrain vehicles, make it easier to overhunt caribou at their traditional crossing places or along their migration routes. All-terrain vehicles, pipelines, heavy-duty machines and even footprints may rip up the thin layer of vegetation and make mud of the permafrost, destroying feeding or nesting grounds. These tracks can remain for a hundred years or more.

Sometimes the trouble comes from elsewhere. Merlins and sharp-shinned hawks pick up pesticides in southern feeding grounds. Lichen, which provides food for caribou and hence people, is being contaminated by radioactive materials blown in from far away. Arctic water is threatened by oil spills, Arctic atmosphere by industrial chemicals, Arctic land by unsafe and unsightly wastes and Arctic marine mammals by toxic metals, all of which blow in, drift in, or are brought in from somewhere else. And in the cold, dry Arctic climate, pollutants don't rot, evaporate or go away.

Canada's federal government is putting in place an Arctic Environmental Strategy to help protect the NWT's fragile ecosystem. In a sense, the wilderness and wildlife of the NWT belong to all the peoples of the world. Individuals from many countries are trying to help conserve this masterpiece of nature. By preserving this relatively pristine part of our planet, perhaps we can learn how to restore and preserve the rest of the world.

These deep tire tracks gouged into the land may still be there years, even decades, from now, demonstrating all too clearly how vulnerable tundra vegetation is.

CHAPTER FOUR

The People

S ixty-one percent of the residents of the NWT are Inuit or Inuvialuit (formerly known as Eskimos), Dene (Indians), or Métis (of Dene and European ancestry). This high proportion of aboriginals in the community makes the NWT unique and is essential to its character.

The Dene

The Dene who live in the NWT have certain similarities in language and culture to Indians who live in Alaska, British Columbia, Alberta and New Mexico. They all speak Athapaskan languages, most of which have a word similar to *Dene* meaning "people."

One Dene story says that, at the beginning of time, an old Dene travelled eastward from the mountains (the Rockies) and arrived at the Big River (the Mackenzie). He caught a multitude of fish and happily returned to his relatives and friends. Many then moved their camps to the Big River. Others crossed the Big River to get to Sahtu (Great Bear Lake) and the Barren Lands.

This story is not too different from the theory put forward by scientists who believe that about 10 000 years ago the ancestors of modern Dene moved eastward from Alaska and the Yukon to follow the caribou. They add that about 7000 years ago, as the glaciers of the last ice age retreated, hunters from the south followed the caribou in their summer migration onto the tundra. Small flint tools, bone scrapers and other evidence dug up near Fort Liard tell us that the ancestors of the modern Dene had a fishing camp there for 9000 years.

Traditional ways live on: *(clockwise)* Dene drummer; teepee at sunset on the Slave River; making birchbark baskets at Nahanni Butte; storyteller John Blondin.

By about 2500 years ago, the Dene had spread across the Subarctic forests and tundra, forming various groups, developing various languages, and evolving slightly different ways of life. The main groups were the Yellowknife Chipewyan, who are now extinct; the Caribou Chipewyan; the Dogribs; the Slaveys; the Mountain and Nahanni Indians, who have now merged with the lowland Slaveys; the North Slaveys and Sahtu people, on Great Bear Lake; and the Tetlit Gwich'in around the Mackenzie Delta.

Until recently, the lifestyle of all these Dene was generally the same. They travelled constantly in small family groups, following

the seasonal movements of the particular animals in their territory —
moose, bison, caribou, sheep, goat, rabbit, beaver. They hunted them
with bows and arrows, spears, clubs, snares and deadfalls. They caught
fish in stone weirs, in baskets or nets made of willow bark, or by jigging
them with hook and line. In winter they set nets under the ice.

In summer, family groups travelled in canoes made from birchbark,
sprucebark or moosehide. In winter they walked on snowshoes,
carrying their gear in packsacks, or they drove teams of dogs pulling
toboggans. While on the move, they made do with brush lean-tos or
bark shelters, but when they stayed in one place, they put up teepees
covered with caribou skin or moose hide.

The Dene had a hard life, and groups were often at war with each
other. But they did have time to relax — usually in summer — and then
they would gather together in a good hunting and fishing place to share
food, hold contests, play gambling games, tell stories and sing and
dance in a circle to the beat of a skin drum. They would also pray and
make offerings to the fire to celebrate their relationship with the land.

The Dene were very much in tune with the physical and spiritual
world around them. Their lives depended on it. They believed that each
person had his or her own medicine, or special powers to do certain
things such as healing, predicting the future, or controlling the weather,
animals or people. Some people had stronger medicine than others.

The Inuit

About 10 000 years ago, people called the Paleo-Eskimo, distant
ancestors of the modern Inuit, settled in Alaska. About 4000 years ago,
some of them, called the Pre-Dorset people, travelled eastward across
the Arctic as far as Greenland, and southward as far as Great Slave
Lake. They hunted seal, walrus and caribou with tools made of stone,
bone, antler or anything they could find.

Their way of life evolved into what archeologists call the Dorset
culture, so named because evidence of it was first unearthed around
Cape Dorset on Baffin Island. It flourished between 1000 B.C. and

One of several mounds found on an island in the Burnside River. They are believed to be the remains of Inuit dwellings dating from the Little Ice Age, 1400-1700. Stone foundations support dome-like walls and roofs built by entwining hundreds — in one case 4000 — of caribou antlers.

A.D. 1000. The Dorset people are best known for their tiny, intricate carvings and the winter igloos they built from spiralling blocks of snow.

About a thousand years ago, a second group of immigrants came east from Alaska — the Thule, who are the direct ancestors of today's Inuit. The Indians, who regarded these newcomers as enemies, called them Eskimos, which means "eaters of raw flesh" in the Chipewyan language. But like the Dene, the modern Inuit prefer to use the names they call themselves: Inuit, for those who live in the Eastern Arctic, and Inuvialuit, for those who live in the Western Arctic. Both words mean "people." Inuk and Inuvialuk mean "person."

Unlike the nomadic Dorset people, the Thule lived in fairly permanent villages along the coastline where they hunted whales. They picked up the idea of snow houses from the Dorset but introduced new things such as the harpoon; the hunting kayak; the large, open woman's boat called an *umiak;* the *komatik,* or sled pulled by dogs.

Between 1650 and 1850, there was a little ice age during which many of the whales disappeared. Some Thule moved inland and farther south to hunt caribou. Their descendants, the people west of Baker Lake, are the only inland Inuit in the NWT. The coastal Thule abandoned their large villages and became nomads travelling in family groups.

At that time evolved the way of life that today's Inuit adults

The old ways and the new. *Far left:* Carver at work in skin tent. *Left:* Bathurst Inlet, where the Inuit still live off the land, very much as their ancestors did. *Below:* Schoolroom at Cape Dorset, with teacher's baby an accepted part of the scene

remember. In spring and early summer they camped in skin tents, fished for char, and hunted seals, walrus and whales. Later in the season, they travelled inland to spear musk-oxen or scare caribou into water or ravines with *inukshuks*, huge piles of stones that look like people. In fall the Inuit fished, stored food and sewed skin clothing, including double suits of caribou fur. In winter they lived in snow houses or circular, half-buried sod and stone houses with roofs made from whalebone or caribou antler covered in skins. They caught wolves, foxes, hares and even polar bears in stone traps at any time of the year.

The Inuvialuit, who lived in the Mackenzie Delta, had better hunting territory. They maintained the old Thule tradition of hunting beluga whales and still have many links with Alaska.

Life for the Inuit and Inuvialuit centred on the family, including parents, grandparents, children and often married children. Decisions were made by consensus, or agreement, and certain people, such as shamans, had medicine power.

The Native way of life continued unaltered until Europeans came. Then changes were inevitable, but much of the traditional life continues in the NWT. Ways vary from one community to another, but the family unit remains central. People still prefer and share country foods; they still wear moccasins, *mukluks* and mitts; their artists use traditional designs; drum dances and gambling games are part of most community events; and government functions in the Native way, by consensus.

The Métis

When Europeans settled in Canada, many of them married Native women, and their offspring were called Métis. Métis pride themselves on being independent and being able to live in two worlds. Indeed, they had two cultures to enrich their lives. This made them very important in the fur trade as intermediaries, interpreters and traders. They were also keen river pilots and businesspeople, as well as skilled hunters, paddlers and packers.

The first Métis people to settle in the NWT were French-speaking voyageurs who paddled with Alexander Mackenzie and supported

Right: **Versatile Métis artist Marvin Bourque and some of his works.**
Far right: **Like most northern mothers, Irene Tagoona takes her baby along in her amouti just about anywhere she goes — even fishing.**

John Franklin's party on their inland explorations. As the fur trade expanded, many European (often Scottish) fur traders married Dene women, had large families and stayed. Other Métis came north from Manitoba, Saskatchewan and Alberta after the failure of Louis Riel's Northwest Rebellion. Today most Métis live around Great Slave Lake and the Mackenzie River, their original homes.

Non-Natives

The number of non-Natives in the NWT increased dramatically in the 1970s and 1980s. They came to make money, get experience, find adventure, help Native people — or do all four. The majority worked for government or industry and enjoyed considerable financial benefits to compensate for the isolation and high cost of living. Most were bureaucrats (civil or public servants), teachers, nurses, and police officers. Others were professionals (doctors, dentists, lawyers, architects), technicians, business entrepreneurs, tradespeople, or rotating crews of miners and oil riggers.

They went to where the jobs were — the urban administration or industrial centres of Yellowknife, Hay River, Fort Smith, Inuvik, Norman Wells and Iqaluit. A few — nurses, teachers, RCMP officers, priests and top government administrators — went to the smaller communities. Most meant to stay awhile, save money then go south to spend it.

That trend has been changing. Fewer non-Natives are migrating to the NWT, more who do migrate are marrying into Native families, and many non-Natives, their children and grandchildren are settling permanently in the North. Whether this trend lasts remains to be seen, however, as an Affirmative Action Policy now in place means that a Native is likely to be chosen over a non-Native when both apply for the same job.

For the moment, the NWT still depends heavily on non-Natives. This won't change until Native students decide to stay in school longer and train to fill skilled positions presently held by non-Natives.

CHAPTER FIVE

Early Adventurers

The first Europeans to travel to the NWT were probably the Vikings, Norsemen who sailed west to Greenland about a thousand years ago. They likely visited Baffin Island, which they named Helluland.

Much later, between 1576 and the late 1800s, British explorers came in large, wooden sailing ships. They were searching for the Northwest Passage, a water route north of the continent that they hoped would be a shortcut to the riches of the Orient. They also hoped their exploits would gain them fame, fortune and a place in the history books. Some sought the North Pole. At that time, people believed that there was open sea around the pole. Instead, there was ice: slow-moving, impenetrable mountains of ice, sometimes three times higher than the explorers' ships. Sailors got to know the pack ice well; many were stuck in it for years at a time.

You'll find the explorers' names all over the map of the NWT: Frobisher, Hudson, Baffin, Davis, Foxe, Ross, Parry, Franklin, McClure and dozens more. The people who paid their way were immortalized, too, including Lady Franklin, Queen Victoria and King William. Most names are British in origin because Great Britain, which claimed sovereignty over the area, sent many explorers.

By the year 2000, probably 12 000 of the present names on the map will be replaced by Native names and 100 000 new names will be added. These changes will reflect the considerable contribution made by Natives during the explorers' journeys — people like Akaitcho, Matonabbee, Kalutunah, Ebierbing and Tookolito.

Scene near the entrance of Hudson Strait, painted by Arctic explorer Sir George Back

Akaitcho, seen here with his son, was chief of the Yellowknife Chipewyan at the time of the first two Franklin expeditions.

Unlike the Dene and Inuit, the British were ill-equipped and either unable or unwilling to live off the land or sea. Many suffered — and died — from a combination of darkness-induced depression, unsuitable clothing, lack of proper nutrition, lead poisoning, boredom, inadequate shelter and the exhausting effort of trying to pull their ships and heavy sleds through the ice.

John Franklin, the best known of the explorers, made three expeditions to the NWT seeking the Northwest Passage. During two of them (1819-22 and 1825), he explored the Arctic coast by travelling up the Coppermine and Mackenzie rivers; on the third (1845-48), he tried to go by sea through the Arctic Islands. Franklin finally found one of several possible Northwest Passages, but he and all of his 128 men perished, most while trying desperately to flee their ice-bound ships. In 1859, a mound of stones was discovered on King William Island containing a written record of their deaths. Much remains a mystery.

The RCMP ship *St. Roch* battles Arctic ice in 1940 on its way to becoming the first ship to sail the Northwest Passage from west to east.

Forty expeditions travelled through the Arctic over a dozen years looking for clues to Franklin's disappearance. Others made scientific observations. As a result, more of the NWT was mapped, more Inuit were contacted, and Canada claimed sovereignty over the Arctic.

It wasn't until 1906 that the Northwest Passage was successfully navigated in its entirety — by a Norwegian, Roald Amundsen in his ship *Gjoa* — and not until 1909 that someone finally reached the geographic North Pole — both Robert Peary and Frederick Cook claimed to be first. In 1940 the RCMP schooner *St. Roch,* captained by Sergeant Henry Larsen, became the first vessel to go all the way through the Northwest Passage in a single season.

Since 1940 hundreds of other adventurers have mounted expeditions through the Northwest Passage or to the North Pole, all seeking different ways to do it first. They have tried the passage in all kinds of boats from rubber to steel; they have tried to reach the Pole by dogsled and dirigible, snowmobile and icebreaker, submarine and bush plane, motorcycle and dogteam, skis and on foot. In 1992 four men tried to ski to the Pole and back again just as Peary and Cook said they had — that is, without the help of airlifted supplies or electronic navigation. Two of them almost succeeded — an extraordinary feat.

Fur Traders

Meanwhile, fur traders, who sought profit rather than glory, were approaching the NWT from the south. First the Hudson's Bay Company, and then its rival, the North West Company, were set up to trade with the Natives for fur.

Dene of the Great Slave Lake area come to trade at Fort Resolution. For a long time, trading operated on a credit system, with the trader providing trappers with what they needed to outfit their winter trapping and the trappers returning in spring to pay their debts with furs. *Insets:* **Explorers Samuel Hearne** *(left)* **and Alexander Mackenzie** *(right)* **played a major role in opening the northern interior to the fur trade.**

Between 1770 and 1772, Samuel Hearne of the Hudson's Bay Company, aided by his Chipewyan guide, Matonabbee, travelled inland on foot from Hudson Bay to the Arctic coast along the Coppermine River. He was looking for copper and a means of trading directly with the Natives who had it. He found little copper and no practicable trade route.

In 1789 Alexander Mackenzie, working for the North West Company, set out to find a navigable route from Lake Athabasca to the Pacific Ocean. Helped by French-Canadian voyageurs and a Chipewyan Dene known as English Chief, he travelled from Fort Chipewyan, on Lake Athabasca, to Great Slave Lake, then down the river that now bears his name. On finding that the Mackenzie led to the Arctic Ocean and not to the Pacific, he called it the "River of Disappointment." Both Hearne and Mackenzie failed to achieve their immediate goals, but their discoveries greatly increased European knowledge of the northern interior.

After years of bitter rivalry, the North West Company finally amalgamated with the Hudson's Bay Company in 1821, and the fur trade rapidly expanded. Trading posts such as Fort Resolution, Fort Liard, Fort Good Hope, Arctic Red River and Fort McPherson are among those that still exist as communities today. Others were abandoned and are now buried in the bush.

Communication improved slowly; York boats and then steamers replaced canoes on the larger inland waterways, and steamships replaced sail for carrying furs and supplies across the Atlantic. Despite improved transportation — a railway reached Calgary by 1880 — the inland route was long; it sometimes took two to three years for parcels to reach their destinations.

Traders led lonely lives, but they kept busy hunting, fishing, growing food, chopping wood for fuel and exploring. They were more than traders. They found themselves providing food, medical care, mail service, transportation, counselling and law enforcement.

The early 1900s were boom years for the fur trade. Prices were high and furs were abundant, so more and more white people came north to trap and trade. By the end of the 1930s, the fur trade had declined in the South, but it continued to develop for a time in the North.

The Whalers

While fur traders came into Dene territories, whalers came into Inuit lands. The gigantic bowhead whales that thronged the waters off Baffin Island and the Mackenzie Delta were rich sources of bone and oil, valuable items before the days of steel, rubber and petroleum. In those days, a bowhead whale was worth $100 000, so whaling was a lucrative business.

American and European whalers were killing whales commercially by 1818 in the Eastern Arctic and by 1889 in the Western Arctic. They killed every whale they could get, and by the turn of the century, the bowhead whale was almost extinct.

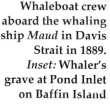

Whaleboat crew aboard the whaling ship *Maud* in Davis Strait in 1889. *Inset:* Whaler's grave at Pond Inlet on Baffin Island

Just as fur traders set up trading posts, whalers set up shore stations. Some of the most important were Herschel Island in the west, and Kekerten Island and Marble Island in the east. These are now preserved as historic sites or territorial parks.

The whole whaling industry fell apart when the number of whales declined and petroleum products became available. All at once, the fur trade above the tree line began to flourish. Former whaling captains stayed to open independent trading posts, some on land and others on boats. The "floating posts" travelled along the coast trading for furs out of sheltered harbours. The Hudson's Bay Company opened many posts throughout the North, too.

The Effects of Contact

Dependence on the trading post changed the Inuit and Dene ways of life. Trapping became their tradition along with hunting and fishing. The Dene remained nomadic until about 1900. They usually came to the posts during spring and fall to trade their furs for goods such as blankets, axes, firearms, tea, flour and rum.

As the Dene began to settle around the fur-trading posts, so the Inuit gathered around the shore stations. The Inuit supplied meat and clothing to the whalers and their families, crewed and captained whale boats and grew increasingly dependent on their goods and weapons. The whalers' influence on the Native way of life was considerable because they came in great numbers, stayed year round, encouraged the Inuit to work for wages, introduced them to alcohol and exposed them to disease.

As time went on, some Inuit who had exclusive hunting, trapping and trading rights in certain areas bought schooners and former whaling boats to become fur traders. The Bankslanders, for instance, travelled by schooner between Banks Island and Aklavik, trapping white fox on the island in winter and selling them on the mainland in summer. Several Inuit families became very wealthy.

Others were not so lucky. The most immediate harm done was

the decimation of the Native peoples by diseases brought by the fur traders and whalers. Aboriginals had no natural protection against foreign diseases, so measles, smallpox, influenza and tuberculosis spread quickly through their populations. Thousands of Inuit and Dene died — whole families, sometimes whole communities.

But some say greater harm was caused by the gradual changes to the Native way of life and the loss of ancient traditions. This may be true, but for the most part the more isolated Inuit and Dene have survived the non-Native invasion of North America far better than their cousins to the south.

Missionaries

Where the fur traders and whalers went, Anglican and Roman Catholic missionaries soon followed. These brave people dedicated their lives to bringing the Christian religion to the non-Christian peoples of the North. Although they sometimes did more harm than good, they had the best of intentions.

Missionaries were great travellers, explorers and mapmakers, trekking vast distances by snowshoe, dog team and canoe. They needed to be independent and versatile. They had to build their own homes and churches, hunt and fish for themselves and their dogs, grow food, get their own fuel, tend the sick, and travel from camp to camp in the bush and over the tundra in all seasons to find their congregations. Many also found time to learn the Native languages, translate books, keep detailed journals, do archeological research, and record the Native way of life.

Reverend Edmund Peck introduced writing to the Inuit through syllabics, a method whereby each symbol represents one syllable. A similar system was designed by Father Émile Petitot; both are still used in the NWT. Legends grew around some of the missionaries. One, for instance, was famous for living in an ice cave; another, who experienced many hardships during his northern travels, was nicknamed "The Bishop Who Ate His Boots."

Left: **Anglican church at Tuktoyaktuk.** *Right:* **Oblate missionaries during the first ordination of a priest ever held in the NWT. Note the Dene motifs on the robes.**

The first schools, convents, hostels, hospitals and seniors' homes in the NWT were built by the Oblate Missionaries and the Grey Nuns. At the Fort Providence and Fort Simpson missions, the missionaries grew crops and raised cattle in addition to running schools and hospitals.

Missionaries have been criticized for their strict discipline, for taking Native children from their families for long periods of time, and for teaching them an alien way of life. By imposing their own culture on Native people, missionaries sometimes caused them to lose touch with their own beliefs and traditions. However, the missionaries did what they thought best at the time, and many Native leaders value the schooling the missions provided. Also, much that was wrong has been corrected, so that now many churches respect Native ways and traditions, and many Natives have taken the Christian religion into their hearts and lives.

CHAPTER SIX

Opening the North

In 1870 the new Dominion of Canada assumed sovereignty over all the land that is now mainland NWT, as part of an even larger territory that included more than half of present-day Canada. As years passed, chunks of what was then called the North-West Territories were carved out to make Yukon, Saskatchewan and Alberta, and to expand Manitoba, Ontario and Quebec.

Throughout most of this time, the Dominion of Canada did little about governing the vast "leftover" territory. Only in the early 1900s did the rest of Canada begin to notice the north country. Foreign whalers were staying in the Arctic all winter long; would-be gold miners were battling to get to the Yukon or staking claims around Great Slave Lake and the Liard and Nahanni river valleys; explorers from other countries were crisscrossing the Arctic, making maps, asking questions and raising flags. The government of Canada decided that it was time to support its own claims with action.

Police and Government Officers

Police officers provided the first real government in the NWT. In 1903 the North-West Mounted Police (NWMP) — later renamed the Royal Canadian Mounted Police (RCMP) — set up their first permanent posts at whaling stations on Herschel Island and Fullerton Island, and at Fort McPherson. More followed as fur-trading posts increased in number and size. Commonly, a line of buildings appeared along a waterfront: the blue and white Mounted Police detachment, the red and white HBC post and the Roman

The Dempster, one of the world's most spectacular highways

Right: Search party preparing to set out from Dawson on February 28, 1911, to look for the Lost Patrol. *Below:* The whole world heard about the RCMP during its long pursuit of Albert Johnson, "The Mad Trapper of Rat River," in the winter of 1931-32. Seen here are some of the RCMP officers involved, with famous bush pilot Wop May on the far right.

Catholic and Anglican mission buildings, which were usually green and white.

But the NWMP didn't stay put. Like the traders and missionaries, they travelled huge distances by dogteam on regular patrols. The one exception to their remarkably successful record of travel and exploration was the Lost Patrol of 1911. Inspector Fitzgerald and his three companions became lost and starved to death on their way from Fort McPherson to Dawson City. A search party, led a few months later by Corporal W.J. Dempster, found the frozen bodies. The Dempster Highway, which is named after the corporal, follows his route.

Government representatives, called Indian Agents, first came to the western NWT at Fort Simpson and Fort Smith, in 1911. Their main job was to provide government to the Natives, but as one elder explains, "They took care of everything." In the eastern NWT, where government administration came later, the agents were called Northern Service Officers.

Establishing Treaties

The Yukon Gold Rush of 1898 and the discovery of oil near Fort Norman in 1920 prompted the government of Canada to make treaties with the Native peoples. Its purpose was to establish its ownership of the land so that it could control the resources and ensure that law and order were maintained when more people arrived. Treaty 8, signed in 1899 with the Cree and Chipewyan, covered the land south of Great Slave Lake, and Treaty 11, signed in 1921 with the Slavey, Dogrib, Hare and Loucheux (Gwich'in), covered the Mackenzie Valley. No treaties were signed with the Inuit.

There is much difference of opinion now about what those treaties meant. The government of Canada considers that the Dene gave up ownership of their traditional lands and the right to control them. The actual words read: "The said Indians do hereby cede, release, surrender and yield up to the Government of the Dominion of Canada, for her Majesty the Queen and her successors for ever, all their rights, titles and privileges whatsoever." In return, the Natives would have the right to continue hunting, trapping and fishing, subject to government regulations, forever.

In addition to what was written in the treaties, the government also promised the Natives free education, free medicine and general assistance when necessary; no taxation, no enforced military service and no interference in their religion; and the assignment of a fair portion of land to them when settlement advanced and they required it.

Although the Dene chiefs signed the treaties, Dene today have their own interpretation of what they meant and mean. Elders insist they never gave up the land because, in their philosophy, nobody owns land. They say the treaties were simply "peace and friendship" agreements, by which Natives allowed others to use the land and were themselves left to continue their traditional way of life.

These opposing points of view are of critical importance now, as the government tries to settle Dene and Métis land claims. However,

Above: Treaty Day Feast at Fort Rae in 1939. *Right:* Treaty Days are still held every summer in Dene communities. As part of the ceremony, every member of the community receives a small token of money, symbolic of the Dene's historic exchange with the government.

at the time of the signing, the treaties were respected as official agreements, and the Native peoples accepted newcomers into their lands peacefully.

Pilots and Miners

Bush pilots made it easier for people to come into the NWT. In 1921 two aircraft, F-13 Junker monoplanes on their way to the oil fields north of Fort Norman, flew into Fort Simpson. These were the first aircraft to fly into the NWT. One crash-landed, and the engine of the other one seized. The men managed to fly out a month later with a propeller made from dogsled planks and the glue of boiled moose hides. Eight years later, Punch Dickins landed at Aklavik, becoming the first pilot to fly north over the Arctic Circle. Wop May, Grant McConachie, Max Ward, Weldy Phipps and Willy Laserichs are a few of the many legendary names in NWT aviation.

The bush pilot became the new hero of the NWT, shortening months of canoe and dogteam travel to days. Flying by the seat of their pants, making daring decisions and homespun repairs, they

Pilots stranded at Fort Simpson in 1921 land safely after testing their home-made propeller.

explored largely unknown country without radios, maps or weather forecasts. In the 1920s, two-way radio became standard aircraft equipment; weather-stations and direction-finding stations were established and gradually expanded. But even today's pilots need courage and ingenuity to deal with the NWT's unpredictable weather, rugged terrain and vast distances.

Air transport made it easier for prospectors and miners to come into the country and establish communities. In 1921 oil discoveries and an on-the-spot refinery led to a new community called Norman Wells. The town of Port Radium sprang up in 1930 when pitchblende, from which radium and uranium are mined, was discovered at Great Bear Lake. In 1933 gold was discovered in Yellowknife Bay, and within three years Yellowknife was a boom town. In 1955 a nickel mine was established in Rankin Inlet on Hudson Bay, and in 1957 a lead-zinc mine was opened at Pine Point near Great Slave Lake. Communities began to grow around the mining camps.

Soldiers and Construction Workers

Before the Second World War, newcomers only trickled into the NWT; during the war, they flooded in. Thousands of American soldiers and Canadian construction workers streamed north to prepare defence installations in case of an attack by Japan or Germany. They built roads, pipelines and airfields. They also expanded the traditional marine transportation system along the Athabasca, Slave and Mackenzie rivers.

Construction crews moved laboriously over frozen land and water in long lines of tracked vehicles called cat trains. These were giant homes on wheels that included kitchens and bedrooms. They bulldozed winter roads out of the ice and snow. They built all-weather gravel roads, with ferries to bridge major rivers, including the first rough road from Grimshaw, Alberta, to Hay River on Great Slave Lake.

Postwar Development

After the Second World War, most of the soldiers left, but the roads they had built encouraged more people to come to the NWT — more miners, more construction workers and more government administrators.

"Roads to Resources" was the battle cry of Prime Minister John Diefenbaker in the 1950s. "We intend to start a vast roads program for the Yukon and Northwest Territories which will open up for exploration vast new oil and mineral areas....Sir John A. Macdonald saw Canada from East to West. I see a new Canada — a Canada of the North!"

In the 1950s and 1960s, more all-weather roads were built. In 1978 the Dempster Highway reached Inuvik, giving the Yukon its first road connection to the NWT. A winter ice road continues to Tuktoyaktuk. In 1984 the Liard Highway between Fort Nelson on the Alaska Highway and Fort Simpson gave British Columbia its first all-weather connection with the NWT.

Although Canadian National Railways (CN) built a railway line from Alberta to the lead-zinc mine of Pine Point in 1965, miners and most other people now use air transportation to reach the NWT. Almost all communities are linked by either scheduled or charter air service.

A lone car travels the ice road that in winter extends the Dempster Highway to Tuktoyaktuk. *Inset:* Road sign on the Liard Highway at the turnoff to Wrigley and the unfinished Mackenzie Highway.

CHAPTER SEVEN

The Growth of Communities

In the 1950s, the United States paid for the building of the Distant Early Warning Line (the DEW line), a chain of airfields and radar stations scattered across northern NWT from Alaska to Greenland. Its function was to detect potential enemy air attacks from over the North Pole. The DEW line has since been modernized and is now called the North Warning System. Although the United States shares in the cost, it is constructed, operated and maintained by Canadians.

The construction of the DEW Line brought many people into the NWT and changed the traditional hunting and trapping economy into a modern wage economy. Many southerners came north to work on the DEW line and many Inuit left their homes to seek employment at the construction sites. Their families followed. Hall Beach is one community that developed in 1955 as a direct result of the DEW line. Others, such as Cambridge Bay, were trading posts that rapidly expanded.

Creating Communities

When the DEW line construction ended, so did the employment, but few Natives went back to camp living. They were now accustomed to modern technology. They wanted cash to buy the things that made their lives easier, such as snowmobiles, boats and kickers (motors). They also wanted to be close to their children in the mission schools or hostels. Instead of just visiting the trading post, more and more came to settle there permanently. The government of Canada encouraged the growth of communities. In some cases it started them.

Hall Beach, on the eastern shore of the Melville Peninsula

Pond Inlet. The arrangement of community buildings and houses in lines facing the shore is typical of many northern towns. *Inset above:* New North Warning System radar station on Brevoort Island. *Inset right:* Town Centre, Cambridge Bay

The 1950s were hard times for many people in the NWT, especially Native people. Fur prices were low, caribou herds had strayed from their usual migration routes, an epidemic killed most of the sled dogs and tuberculosis was widespread. Many people died of starvation and disease.

In response to these disasters, the federal government moved people into communities where it could more easily provide food, houses and, if possible, work. In moving families from Quebec and Pond Inlet to Grise Fiord and Resolute Bay, the government also hoped to solidify Canadian ownership of the High Arctic.

In the 1960s, the government, which had been subsidizing church schools, hostels and hospitals, now began building its own. It also built houses, government offices, post offices, power plants and airports. Later, it constructed community halls, recreation centres, libraries and senior citizens' complexes. It had to start from scratch and it had to work quickly, especially in the east, where the Inuit were just starting to come in from the land.

The face of the North changed drastically and with great speed. As a result, many communities look alike. The store, church and police buildings line the waterfront as they always did. Behind them, on flat ground or terraced gravel, are long lines of box-shaped bungalows spaced far apart so that trucks can get in and out to deliver water and pick up garbage and sewage. The first houses were called "matchboxes" because they were tiny and caught fire easily. Later the government built larger, two-storey houses in a variety of styles, but transportation costs and the problems of building on permafrost continue to limit the range of designs that can be used.

Community Problems

Soon there were a lot of buildings, but what were Native people to do? Strangers — traders, priests, police officers, game wardens, teachers, nurses, doctors, social workers and dozens of other government personnel — had taken on the responsibilities that had once been those of hunters, parents, elders, medicine men and tribal councils.

Well-meaning government officials stifled any sense of responsibility; the physical structure of the community made traditional activities difficult; modern technology made life too easy; and the welfare system made people dependent. Who wanted to freeze in the bush or on the tundra when a warm bed, store-bought food and a television set awaited in town? Idleness and the constant challenge of trying to cope with both the old and the new have led to many social problems in the NWT.

Co-operatives

In the late 1950s, people started two movements for providing income, solving social ills and nurturing pride in their traditions. The first movement draws on the unique artistic talent of the Inuit. After recognizing the quality of the small carvings many Inuit made for themselves, James Houston started a government-sponsored arts-and-crafts centre at Cape Dorset, on Baffin Island. He encouraged people to carve large pieces of soapstone, which would appeal to buyers down south, and taught them engraving and print-making techniques. Other communities were inspired to encourage local artists.

Almost every community also has a Native-owned co-operative store, or co-op, as they are commonly known. This second movement, too, has provided employment and pride in traditional ways. Co-operatives are multi-purpose operations that sell just about everything including Native arts and crafts. But they may also be involved in delivering water, fuel oil or freight; running hotels, fishing lodges or taxi services; doing construction and

Right: Inuit sculptures. *Far Right:* Collecting soapstone at Markham Bay on Baffin Island. Once a year, Inuit dynamite a hill of soapstone at low tide, then at high tide transport it by boat and stockpile it on the tundra for winter snowmobile pickup.

maintaining buildings. These community-owned co-ops are usually run by Natives, and profits go back into the business or community. Outside of government, co-ops are the single largest employer of Native people in the NWT. The arts-and-crafts industry and the co-operative movement, both of which are built on traditional ways of thinking, are NWT success stories.

Native Development Corporations

In the interest of increasing Native involvement in the community, over 50 Native development corporations have recently been established. These corporations enable Natives to get more training in business management and to take advantage of more business opportunities, especially in the investment of land-claims money. They are buying existing businesses, going into joint ventures and investing in hotels, airlines and petroleum companies. Most have non-Native advisers or management.

Co-op store in Igloolik

CHAPTER EIGHT
Government

Although the NWT does not have provincial status, it nonetheless sends elected representatives to Parliament in Ottawa, and it governs itself through a legislative assembly.

The Birth of Government

Until 1967 the NWT was governed by an appointed non-Native commissioner and a mostly non-Native council that was first appointed and later partly elected. They were based in Ottawa and reported to the Department of Indian Affairs and Northern Development, an administrative branch of the federal government.

Then, on September 18, 1967, a planeload of federal government workers touched down in Yellowknife, the newly declared capital, to run the NWT. Within 25 years, that planeload of bureaucrats had increased to nearly 10 000 — one government worker for every 16 persons in the population.

The chief executive officer for the new government in Yellowknife was Commissioner Stu Hodgson, whose nickname, Emperor of the Arctic, reflected his near total authority. During the next 12 years, Hodgson actively promoted the NWT to the world, and the role of government to the NWT people. He encouraged northerners to seek responsible, northern-controlled government with their own elected representatives.

Legislative Assembly of the Northwest Territories in session, 1991

From 1979 to 1989, under the guidance of Commissioner John Parker, the legislative assembly became the most powerful political body. It was made up of elected representatives, and had an elected executive council (later called a cabinet). The elected head of the assembly is known as the government leader.

As the powers of the elected members increased, those of the commissioner decreased. In 1989 Dan Norris became the first northerner and the first Native to be appointed commissioner. Unlike the first commissioner, he has no direct political power.

Only since 1962 has the NWT been represented in the federal government. In 1992 the two members of Parliament in Ottawa were both Native: Ethel Blondin-Andrew, a Dene, for the Western Arctic and Jack Anawak, an Inuk, for the Eastern Arctic. The NWT has one representative in the Senate, Willie Adams, an Inuk.

By 1992, 18 of the 24 elected members of the legislative assembly were Native and the government leader was an Inuvialuk: Nellie Cournoyea, the first Native and the first woman to be elected as head of a government in Canada. In 1992 the leader of the NWT finally became a full participant in a first ministers' conference.

Local Government

The territorial government of the NWT is often referred to as the GNWT. But there are other levels of government as well. Just as the federal government continues to transfer many province-like responsibilities to the territorial government, so does the GNWT transfer increasing responsibilities to local governments.

Because of the NWT's vast size, the GNWT has five administrative regions, each with its own headquarters: Fort Smith, Inuvik, Kitikmeot, Keewatin and Baffin. Yellowknife, the capital, is in some ways treated as a region in its own right.

By 1992 the NWT had 1 city, 4 towns, 2 villages, 36 hamlets, 4 settlements or settlement corporations, 14 unincorporated communities, 1 reserve and 26 outpost camps. Only a few people

Left: Yellowknife's modern City Hall reflects the rapid development of a community that achieved city status less than 25 years ago. *Above:* Trout Lake is one of ten NWT communities run by the local band council.

still remain "on the land," that is, outside organized communities. Some of these communities are administered by municipal councils, some by Dene band councils (funded by the federal government), some by territorial regional offices and some by a combination of these. There are also 6 regional or tribal councils, and, to advise the GNWT, 800 boards and agencies. Counting all levels of government, there are about 1500 elected politicians — that is, 1 for every 38 people!

Land Claims

Further complicating government in the NWT is the existence of three more political bodies: the Dene Nation, the Métis Association of the NWT, and the Inuit Tapirisat of Canada (ITC). These three Native organizations seek to achieve outright title for specially selected lands in their regions; cash compensation for other lands; a share of royalties from such resource industries as oil, gas and mining; a stronger voice in land management; stronger hunting, fishing and trapping rights; and, in most cases, self-government.

One of the organizations in the ITC is the Inuvialuit Regional Corporation, which, as the Committee of Original Peoples' Entitlement (COPE), signed its land claims agreement in the Western Arctic in 1984.

Another organization, Tungavik Federation of Nunavut (TFN), signed an accord in 1992 to settle its land claims for the Eastern Arctic. The Inuit will get more than $1 billion over 14 years, and effective control over 2.2 million square kilometres (950 000 square miles), nearly all the area above the tree line. They will actually own about one-sixth of that land, or an area about half the size of Alberta. They expect their new territory and government of Nunavut to come into being by 1999.

By 1992 the Gwich'in and the Sahtu had negotiated their agreement with the federal and territorial governments, but other Dene and Métis groups had as yet to reach an agreement.

Uniqueness

Because the land is so remote, distances so vast, people and languages so varied and history of contact with each other so recent, government in the NWT is both difficult and expensive. Perhaps because of the challenges it faces, it has evolved into a unique institution.

Elections are interesting and residents are interested in them. A higher percentage of the population turns out to vote here than anywhere else in Canada. A 90 percent turnout is not uncommon in some communities (the national average is under 60 percent). And where else would ballot boxes be dropped by helicopter? Or taken by chartered plane to fishing or hunting camps? Where else could illiterate residents vote by marking an "X" beside a photograph of a candidate? Or voting hours be extended because a blizzard made it impossible for people to step outside their homes? And where else could someone win a seat with just 45 supporters?

But the NWT government differs mostly because it operates by consensus. This means that decisions are made in the Native way: before any action is taken, all participants must agree. After the members of the legislative assembly (MLAs) are elected by their constituents, they come together in Yellowknife to choose a leader and a cabinet from among themselves. Then, for any issue, each of the MLAs follows his or her own conscience. Political parties do not exist at this level as they do in the provinces.

Solving Problems

The GNWT has to solve many problems. In proportion to the population, the NWT outstrips the rest of Canada in its high levels of unemployment, illiteracy, school drop-outs, drug and alcohol

Like most NWT schools, this one at Fort Good Hope, named after a respected elder, offers kindergarten through grade 9 classes. With youngsters making up about a third of the population, easier access to education beyond this level is high on the GNWT's list of priorities.

abuse, family violence, crime, suicides, cost of living and dependence on social assistance.

The NWT has the highest birth rate in Canada; about a third of its population is under 17 years of age. Few people possess the skills needed for modern jobs, and most are losing their traditional skills. Even when jobs are available, Native people are often reluctant to leave their communities to take them. To make matters worse, there are not enough people paying taxes to support more services, and not enough money coming in from natural resources to pay for them either.

In hopes of solving some of these problems, the people of the NWT are trying to achieve a new kind of government, one in which the lowest — or community — level is the strongest. They are trying to combine the best of the old with the best of the new. Perhaps they will form a council of elders. Perhaps young offenders will be taught life skills on the land rather than being sent to an institution. Perhaps taxes will be collected in the form of community service or food and firewood rather than money.

Two things are certain: future governments will work to encourage Native language and culture and will sponsor an education system that focuses on northern studies.

Division

In 1992, after much argument and a territory-wide vote, the people of the NWT decided to divide their territory into two sections. The Eastern NWT will be called Nunavut, and the Western NWT may be called the New Western Territory, although it is commonly referred to as Denendeh or Nahendeh.

The Inuit of Nunavut have opted for the same type of government as is presently in place for the entire NWT. With 80 percent of their population Inuit and only 20 percent non-Native, the Inuit are assured of being in control.

However, in the New Western Territory, the non-Native population

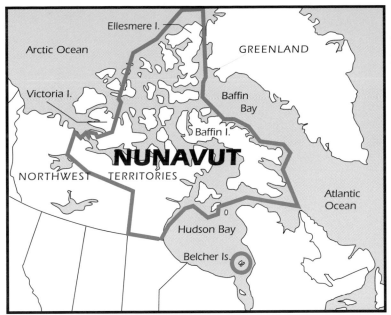

is slightly in the majority (about 52 percent). Dene and Métis make up about 41 percent and the Inuvialuit about 7 percent. Interestingly, the Inuvialuit decided to stay on the western side rather than join their eastern cousins.

With this ethnic mix, what form of government will this "leftover" territory have? A Commission for Constitutional Development suggests that the New Western Territory could be divided into about 15 self-governing districts. The central government in Yellowknife would deal only with matters of mutual concern such as maintaining territory-wide standards and the collection of income tax.

The commission's draft constitution gives special recognition to the role of elders and women in society, and it recognizes the rights of people to refuse medical treatment in favour of traditional Native healing methods and the right to practise midwifery.

One of the difficulties of such a constitution for the 30 000 or so diverse people in the proposed New Western Territory is its cost, its complexity, and the fact that Natives usually pay little or no income tax. Many people are nervous about the future. But whatever happens, these are interesting times for the northern third of Canada.

CHAPTER NINE

Today's Economy

Two kinds of economy operate in today's NWT. In the wage economy, which is most common in urban communities, most people have jobs, and salaries are high. In the subsistence economy of smaller communities, few people earn wages. Instead, most make their living from the land; they depend upon fishing, hunting and trapping to provide food, clothing and a little cash income, which they get from the sale of meat and hides.

One of the weaknesses of the NWT economy is that it imports from the South many more goods than it exports. However, the GNWT has a continuing campaign to persuade residents to "Buy North," and it has a policy of hiring northern businesses to carry out government projects. These two practices should help keep NWT businesses healthy, but in the long term selling more goods to the South is essential.

According to the latest figures, the most valuable industry each year in terms of generating export income is mining, followed by oil and gas, tourism, arts and crafts, sportsfishing, fur production, commercial fishing and sportshunting.

Mining

Minerals and mining have played a big part in the development of the NWT, and they are destined to play an even larger role in its future. Almost every known mineral can be found in the NWT, and geologists have barely scratched the surface. High costs, lack of

The high-tech, ice-breaking cargo ship, *M.V. Arctic,* takes on a load of zinc concentrates at the Polaris zinc and lead mine in the high Arctic.

Left: **Aerial shot of Echo Bay Mines' Lupin gold mine.** *Right:* **A long line of transport trucks make their way along the Lupin Mine winter ice road, with a plow truck in the lead to clear the snow.**

transportation and low prices on the world market delay development, but the GNWT has ambitious plans for overcoming most of these problems.

Apart from government, mining employs more people and brings in more dollars than any other industry. Over 2000 people work in mining-related jobs, and 60 percent of these are northern residents. Mining contributes millions of dollars directly into the NWT economy, and there are many indirect benefits, as well. Although only six mines were working in 1991, they produced 80 percent of the NWT's exports.

Gold is still important in the northern economy. The Lupin gold mine on Contwoyto Lake, just 90 kilometres (56 miles) south of the Arctic Circle, is the world's most northerly gold mine outside Russia. One of Canada's most profitable gold mines, this is a state-of-the-art operation. Lupin's owner, Echo Bay Mines, flew nearly all their materials in by Hercules aircraft — 24 hours a day, 6 days a week, for 20 months. Then they built a 560 kilometre (350-mile) winter ice road across the Barren Lands from Yellowknife to bring in annual supplies. Ice roads are only open for about ten weeks a year, so everything must be trucked in quickly. Otherwise, a whole year is lost. Fortunately, gold bricks go out by air.

The second most northerly mine in the world is the Polaris zinc and lead mine on Little Cornwallis Island, close to the magnetic North Pole. It processes during the year and then ships its stockpiles out on the icebreaker *M.V. Arctic*. Polaris is known as "The Barge" because its mill and accompanying buildings were towed north on a barge from Quebec. At low tide, the whole complex was set down on steel pilings above the Arctic Ocean. Like a hotel, it has an indoor swimming pool, whirlpool and sauna.

The most exciting find in recent years was the 1991 discovery of 81 small diamonds near Lac de Gras. Until then, scientists did not know diamonds could be found in Canada. Many people rushed to the area to stake out their claims — the largest staking rush in Canadian history. So far, they have claimed an area about twice the size of Prince Edward Island.

The Cantung (Canada Tungsten) mine in the Selwyn Mountains is the western world's richest tungsten deposit, but it was shut down in 1985 because of low prices and competition with tungsten mines in China. The town of Tungsten once had 400 people. Now a single family lives there to care for the deserted mine buildings.

There have been many world-class mineral discoveries in the NWT — gold, silver, lead, zinc, copper, uranium and beryllium. But the NWT needs cheaper ways of getting materials in and minerals out before the mining industry can improve. Most people support the government's recent multibillion-dollar Transportation Strategy for building roads across the Barren Lands, establishing a deep-water port on the Arctic coast, and acquiring ships that can ram through the thick ice to extend the shipping season to six months.

Oil and Gas

There are only three active oil and gas fields in the NWT: Bent Horn in the Arctic Islands; Pointed Mountain near Fort Liard; and Norman Wells on the Mackenzie River. But there have been many significant discoveries in the Mackenzie Delta, the Beaufort Sea and the Arctic Islands. The richest so far is Amauligak in the Beaufort Sea.

Offshore areas seem richer in oil, and onshore areas richer in gas. Ironically, there's plenty of gas but not enough gas customers, and there's plenty of oil customers but not enough oil — at least not at a price to warrant getting it to market. So although modern technology allows drilling to go on from artificial islands, ice platforms and ships, there has been little exploration in recent years. The Norman Wells field has had the most success. Oil has been produced there since 1921 and shipped locally by barge. In 1982 the field was expanded considerably by the construction of six artificial islands in the Mackenzie River, and in 1985 a pipeline was built from Norman

About 30 000 barrels of oil a day are pumped south from Norman Wells to Alberta.

Wells to Zama, Alberta, to meet a network of southern pipelines. It was the first fully buried oil pipeline in permafrost.

In 1977 the Berger Report put a 10-year stop to a proposed gas pipeline down the Mackenzie Valley, and one is not expected to be built until at least 2004. The industry is waiting for higher prices and more customers to justify building the $5 billion pipeline; meanwhile, the NWT is waiting for the federal government to give it greater control over oil and gas money and management in an agreement called the Northern Accord.

Renewable Resources

Northerners have been using the renewable resources of the NWT for many years to meet their personal needs. However, the government is now developing these resources commercially.

Trapping and Hunting

The fur trade is the oldest industry in the NWT. It was once the most important as well, but many factors, ranging from changing fashions to the success of anti-trapping lobbies, have weakened it in recent years. Animals presently harvested are mainly beaver, arctic and red fox, lynx, marten, mink, muskrat, wolf and wolverine.

People in small communities eat plenty of country food that they hunt themselves — mainly caribou, moose, musk-ox, seal, whale and birds such as grouse, ptarmigan, duck and goose. In the spirit of traditional ways, people try to use all parts of the animal: meat for food, horns and antlers for carving, musk-ox wool for knitting. To keep more money in the North and boost jobs and income, the government encourages the harvest of game animals and the sale of country foods both at home and for export.

Marine mammals are still hunted for food, clothing and arts-and-crafts supplies, but adverse publicity by animal rights groups has caused the collapse of the sealing industry. However, Nunasi, an Inuit development corporation, is continuing to promote and sell various leather goods made from seal skin under the trade name Amiq Fine Leathers.

Sportshunting is an important industry in the NWT. Hunters come from around the world to hunt big game such as polar bear, musk-ox, caribou, moose and grizzly bear.

Many people in small communities still rely at least partly on traditional activities, such as seal hunting, hide tanning and drying arctic char, to meet their own food and clothing requirements. Increasingly, they are able to sell any surplus for cash.

The NWT is the only place in the world where the polar bear may be legally hunted by non-residents, and sportshunters regard the polar bear hunt as the supreme adventure. Each Inuit village may kill a certain number of bears and can allow sportshunters to hunt some of these. Because each hunter may pay up to $17 000 for a hunt, it is a lucrative way for Inuit to earn money.

Fishing

Fishing is extremely important in the NWT — as a traditional activity and as a commercial industry. To protect the stocks, strict quotas are enforced, and tourists who come to fish for sport are encouraged to release any fish they catch.

Over 50 fishing lodges open each year between June and September. The most popular fishing destinations are Great Bear Lake, Great Slave Lake and Tree River. Sportsfishing probably generates more dollars for the NWT than any other section of the tourism industry.

The three main commercial fisheries are the whitefish fishery on Great Slave Lake and the arctic char fisheries at Cambridge Bay and Rankin Inlet. The GNWT is actively developing valuable new fisheries, such as turbot, shrimp and scallop.

Forestry

The forestry industry is, of course, limited to areas south of the tree line. Although there are 143 000 square kilometres (55 000 square miles) of land covered with useful forest, only 15 percent of the wood northerners use comes from these lands. The GNWT wants to change this. Residents already cut their own wood for heating their homes and building fence posts, but they are being encouraged to buy more home-grown lumber for building. Unfortunately, there are very few sawmills in the NWT.

Many problems plague the forestry, including a shortage of roads and a lack of money and expertise. However, the GNWT is determined to increase production significantly by 1995.

This Lindberg Landing sawmill is one of a very few small sawmills in the NWT.

Right: Raising chickens — a new and successful business at Trout Lake. *Far right:* Greenhouse at Paulatuk, on the Arctic Ocean.

Farming

Yes, there are farms in the NWT — not, perhaps, like the ones on the Prairies, but farms nonetheless. Most of the successful agricultural operations are near Hay River, which has a broiler chicken farm, an egg production farm, a cattle ranch, a fledgling bison ranch and a large market garden. There is more market gardening near Fort Simpson, and Fort Smith has a small cattle ranch. A reindeer herd of about 12 000 animals near Tuktoyaktuk provides reindeer meat and antlers for a small market.

Agriculture now adds comparatively little to the NWT economy. But the government helps boost production by supporting such projects as hydroponic gardening, greenhouses, local community gardens, a silver fox farm, a ptarmigan farm and the making of wild blueberry jam. The NWT Farmers' Association's bold black-and-yellow label proudly reads "NWT Grown." One company, with a polar bear logo on its cartons, sells eggs all across the NWT.

In recent decades, arts and crafts have played a significant role in the NWT economy. Seen here, Inuit printmaker Mary Okheena at Holman and a Dene beadworker

CHAPTER TEN

Culture and Recreation

There's something about the NWT that draws creative people to live here and inspires everybody. Newcomers and Natives alike often feel an urge to communicate what they see and feel up here in a variety of imaginative ways.

Arts and Crafts

One out of every six people in the NWT, and in some communities one out of every two or three, earn money by selling their art — an astonishing statistic.

Wherever you go in the NWT, you'll find people making things. Artists work inside their homes, on the step outside their doors or in a shack on a street. They sell what they have created to visitors who come by, the Northern Store, the local co-op or, in a very few cases, directly to a gallery in the South.

Despite their lack of formal training, Native artists and craftspeople have earned universal respect. Their works can be found all over the world in museums, art galleries and private collections.

When you look at a sample of artwork from the NWT, whether it's a small quillworked box or a monumental sculpture, you get a glimpse of the history, geography and biology of a land, and the autobiography of a people. For Natives, art keeps their culture alive; in the words of one elder, it keeps *them* alive. It provides identity in a fast-changing world.

Dene and Métis, who live below the tree line, use porcupine quills,

Bird with Colourful Plumage **by Kenojuak**

Above: Untitled wall hanging by Jessie Oonark, commissioned for the National Arts Centre in 1973. *Right:* The largest Inuit carving ever made is the *Sedna Legend,* which stands in the lobby of the Hong Kong Bank of Canada in downtown Toronto. Its six life-size figures represent Sedna, the goddess of the sea, Shaman, Polar Bear, Narwhal, Walrus and Seal.

fish scales, moose and caribou hair or beads to make velvet-backed pictures and to decorate clothing, jewellery and birchbark baskets. They carve antler, horn and soapstone, and make replicas of traditional implements: skin drums, sleds, sinew and spruce snowshoes, and moosehide and bark canoes.

Inuvialuit and Inuit, who live above the tree line, carve animals, spirits, and scenes of traditional life from walrus ivory, whalebone, caribou antler and stone. They make traditional games, tools, weapons, drums and goggles from the same natural materials.

Ever adaptive, these two cultures learned from a third: the newcomers' culture. Natives now add metal, glass beads, marble, wool and cotton thread to their already varied materials. They also employ new tools and techniques, such as weaving, print making, oil painting and drilling with power tools. They make wall hangings in woven wool and appliquéd duffle; animal and human dolls of fur and duffle with leather or stone faces; duvets with silkscreened covers; and jewellery in baleen, sealskin, silver and gold. Items from modern life, such as helicopters, oil drums and Christian symbols, sometimes creep into scenes of traditional life.

Far Left: Dene driftwood carving. *Left:* A fine example of moosehair tufting. Traditionally, designs were geometric shapes, but now the pink wild rose, seen here, is the most popular motif.

Clothing is fun as well as functional. The North's long winters are brightened by the vivid colours and varied designs of parkas, jackets, mitts, hats, belts and kamiks (boots). These can be made from furs, cotton and other materials decorated with beads, braid, quills, hair, inlaid fur or appliquéd wool. In the NWT, art is the stuff of life itself.

Different communities specialize in different things. Cape Dorset, the first northern community to achieve artistic success, became world famous for its stone and marble sculptures and its print collection; Baker Lake for its intricately appliquéd wall hangings; Pangnirtung for its woven wool tapestries and tasselled Pang hats; Holman for its floral Mother Hubbard parkas with large "sunburst" fur hoods; Spence Bay, now Taloyoak, for its hand-dyed embroidered parkas and animal dolls with babies in their hoods; Fort Providence for its tufted moosehair pictures; Fort Liard for its birchbark baskets painstakingly decorated with porcupine quills.

Carvings represent 60 percent of all arts and crafts produced in the NWT, but with traditional supplies of serpentine and soapstone in short supply, the GNWT now encourages its artists to use power tools to carve the abundant hard stone.

There are many Métis and non-Native painters in the NWT. Although not as well known internationally as Inuit carvers and printmakers, they record what is left of traditional life and communicate the North's special quality of light and space.

Performing Arts

Because the Native culture grew without a written language, Natives excel at expressing themselves in speech, song and dance. Traditional storytelling, chanting, song duels, throat singing, drum dancing and circle dancing are all central to Native culture, but now so are the fiddling, jigging and square dancing introduced by whalers and traders.

Throat singing is different from anything you've ever heard. Two or three women stand face to face with their mouths close together and make rhythmic noises in their throats and noses. They each use the breath of the others to make their own vocal cords vibrate.

When people meet for a celebration, they usually have a drum dance. Dene drummers stand in line at one end of a room, tapping their drums and chanting songs, while the dancers shuffle around in a circle in a single line. In Inuit drum dancing, only one drummer performs at a time. He stands in the middle of the circle beating each side of his drum in turn as he chants. Another performer carries on when he stops.

Northerners love a good show. A favourite is Susan Aglukark, a singer and storyteller from Arviat, who is now becoming famous in the South. Other popular performers are Inuit folksingers Charlie Panagoniak and Lorna Tassoer of Rankin Inlet; and Jim Green, a poet and storyteller from Fort Smith, and the George Mandevilles, a father-and-son jigging team from Yellowknife.

The Northern Service of the Canadian Broadcasting Corporation (CBC North) has recorded much of the local music. As well, the Northern Arts and Cultural Centre, the Society for Encouragement of Northern Talent, the Department of Culture and Communications and the NWT Arts Council are all very supportive of performing artists in the NWT.

It says much for the natural creativity of NWT performers that Tunooniq Theatre, a successful group of Inuit actors from Igloolik and Pond Inlet, had never seen live theatre before writing and presenting its first play. This group uses traditional storytelling techniques, drum dancing, and ajajaq (chanting) songs to improvise and develop plays on both old and modern themes.

One of Tunooniq Theatre's most popular plays, "Changes," tells about Inuit life before, during and after the coming of the white traders. John Blondin and the Native Theatre Group in Yellowknife do the same thing for the Dene, and the Northern Arts and Cultural Centre there has presented several original plays by local writers.

Left: The Northern Arts and Cultural Centre's production of *Matonabbee. Bottom left:* Performing artists like the Rae Youth Drummers help maintain traditional culture. *Below:* Theatre makes it easier to bridge the gap between cultures and talk out problems. Seen here, the Tunooniq Theatre Group at Pond Inlet.

Left: **Making sand castles on an Arctic beach.** *Bottom left:* **Fort Simpson youngsters enjoy themselves in their quonset hut swimming pool.** *Below:* **Ice-fishing near Yellowknife**

Everyday Fun

Sports and recreation are very important in a land of high unemployment, social problems and long, cold winters. Although most communities in the NWT have fewer than a thousand people, they all have community halls or gyms where local sporting, recreational and cultural activities take place. In addition, most have arenas, curling rinks, playgrounds and playing fields.

Government-sponsored recreation programs have increased tremendously since the early seventies when the world's only travelling pool, "Corky the Barge," stopped at various communities on an annual summer voyage down the Mackenzie River. Now about 20 communities have swimming pools set up in warehouses or quonset huts, which stay open all summer long. A trained, recreational development officer provides services in each community.

People in the NWT are involved in many outdoor activities. In summer they fish, hunt, canoe, boat, hike and camp. In winter they don't let cold temperatures stop them from snowshoeing, cross-country skiing, dog sledding or skidooing. Inuvik runs international curling and skiing championships in spring.

People even play golf in the NWT. It doesn't matter that the greens are sand, tundra or gravel, or that the hazards are ravens — which like to steal golf balls — and blocks of ice that are hard to reach. Yellowknife celebrates the well-known Midnight Sun Golf Tournament in June, but some tournaments are held as far north as Tuktoyaktuk, Holman and Lake Hazen.

Sports Events

Despite the high cost of travel in the NWT, people participate enthusiastically in a number of sports festivals: the Winter Regional Games within the NWT, the Northern Traditional Games held each summer in six regional centres, and the Arctic Winter Games in which NWT athletes compete with athletes from the Yukon, Alaska, Northern Alberta, Greenland and Russia. Northern games festivals are designed to foster cultural knowledge just as much as athletic skills. Bronze, silver and gold medals, all shaped like ulus, the traditional Inuit women's knife, are awarded to the winners.

Northerners play the same sports people down south do, but they have unusual and traditional ones as well. Unlike competitive southern games, in which you play to win and have fixed rules, northern games are tests of individual strength, endurance, skill and patience — all qualities necessary to survive in a harsh environment. Northern games continue until the participants give up.

A few typical Inuit athletic events are arm, finger, ear, mouth and foot pull; head and back push; one- and two-foot high kick; knuckle hop, butt bump and knee walk. These are games suited to long winter days spent in small spaces, such as igloos. In an outside game called blanket toss, everybody holds onto the edge of a circular canvas blanket or walrus hide and tosses the contestant high into the air.

Unlike most Inuit games, Dene games are usually played by teams outside. In pole push, two teams grasp opposite ends of a pole and try to push each other outside a marked ring. It's like tug-of-war in reverse.

A central event of the summer Traditional Games is the Good Woman Contest. In this popular competition, women test their skills in tea boiling, bannock making, duck plucking, muskrat skinning, seal flensing, fish cutting and sewing. Between events, people visit with one another, help themselves to tea and bannock, taste northern foods and look at arts-and-crafts displays. Afterwards, they jig, sing, drum dance or square dance. Often they play and dance through the night. Traditional Games is more than a sporting event; it is a total cultural experience.

Festivals

Festivals are frequent in the NWT and bring people together over vast distances. Sports are played, but the main focus is on friends and fun. Almost every community has a festival or carnival in spring: Iqaluit's Toonik Tyme, Tuktoyaktuk's Beluga Jamboree,

Right: The high kick, one of the events at the Arctic Winter Games. The Games have been held every two years since 1970. *Far right:* Bertha Ruben has been a top competitor in the Good Woman Contest at every Traditional Games since 1970.

Cambridge Bay's Umingmuk Frolics, Hay River's Ookpik Carnival, Yellowknife's Caribou Carnival, and at least five dozen more.

People play broomball and snow-golf as well as traditional games, and they race dogs and snowmobiles. And, in true northern fashion, they invent new games such as portaging canoes and crossing simulated rivers and canyons in the main street. Corporate Challenge, with events such as passing-the-buck and executive drag, is always a favourite in Yellowknife, the government town.

There is an increasing number of annual music festivals and workshops to showcase northern talent. Some of the best known are Folk on the Rocks in Yellowknife, Great Northern Arts Festival in Inuvik and Midway Lake Music Festival in Fort McPherson.

Literature

Northerners have a saying that if writers come up here for an hour they write a newspaper article; if they stay overnight they write a

Activities for everyone at Yellowknife's Caribou Carnival

magazine article; and if they stay a week they write a book. It's true that many people who never have thought of writing a book anywhere else do get inspired by their experience in the North. Almost all of the early explorers, missionaries and anthropologists published their journals and personal narratives. These often included the first written forms of Native stories. Later, people who visited or worked in the NWT wrote their personal memoirs.

Some Dene and Métis have written books, such as Ted Trindell's *Métis Witness to the North,* John Tsetso's *Trapping Is My Life,* and George Blondin's *When the World Was New.* However, the Inuit have written most of the Native literature in the NWT. This is amazing considering that they had no written language until this century. Reading and writing, initiated by the missionaries, spread quickly among a people for whom speech and picture-making were always very important. Some of the best known Inuit books are Markoosie's *Harpoon of the Hunter* and Alootook Ipellie's *Nipikti, the Old Man Carver.* Michael Kusugak from Rankin Inlet has written three children's books based on his childhood experiences. These are the first books to be published by a southern publisher in Inuktitut syllabics as well as English. The first one, *A Promise Is a Promise,* was written in collaboration with well-known children's writer, Robert Munsch.

Some community organizations on Baffin Island, such as the Igloolik Writers Group and Book Making Project and the Baffin Regional Board of Education, are publishing books by local Inuit authors in Inuktitut. Iglooklik particularly treasures its culture; until recently this community did not allow television.

Earlier Native themes were of traditional life and first contact with white culture. Popular current topics are land claims and the difficulty of combining the best of the old and the new ways. If Native writers continue to publish at the rate they have in the last 30 years, they may soon make their mark on world literature.

The Traditional Camp near Baker Lake is set up each summer to show how Inuit families used to live.

Museums and Galleries

Museum collections help all of us remember our heritage and history. There are many collections of ancient artifacts and culturally significant materials throughout the NWT, but you won't find them in regular museums. Instead, you must look in visitors' centres, churches, schools, band offices, airport terminals, shops and arts-and-crafts centres scattered everywhere. Some displays, such as Traditional Camp near Baker Lake, are set up seasonally. Others are particular community landmarks: Albert Faille's one-room house in Fort Simpson and the half-buried sod houses in Pond Inlet and Clyde River.

   The Prince of Wales Northern Heritage Centre in Yellowknife stands out as the most imposing of NWT museums. Judge Jack Sissons' carvings of the NWT's most famous court cases are displayed in the Yellowknife Courthouse.

   Some art galleries have excellent displays of arts and crafts. Among the best are the Arctic Art Gallery and the Webster Gallery in Yellowknife and Coman Arctic Gallery in Iqaluit.

CHAPTER ELEVEN

Communication

Imagine the population of a small suburb of Toronto sprinkled across an area the size of India. In a land as vast as the NWT, such a small number of people obviously need good communications. Yet the huge distances between communities makes contact both difficult and costly.

Radio

People use radios a lot in the NWT. Out in the bush, they send messages to each other on the Hunters' and Trappers' channel. At home, they send messages, greetings and announcements through CBC North. Some kind of radio is nearly always on in the house or cabin or tent.

The first radio stations, called wireless stations, were built and operated by the military — the Royal Canadian Corps of Signals, a branch of the Department of National Defence.

In 1958 these military stations were taken over by the CBC's Northern Service. CBC North, as it is called now, is unique. Nowhere else in the world does one radio network serve a larger area, cover as many time zones and broadcast in so many languages. And nowhere has one grown so rapidly. People come from around the world to learn how CBC North highlights Native programs and helps to preserve Native cultures.

The most ancient communication device in the Arctic is the *inukshuk*. Built by piling large stones into a shape roughly resembling a human being, inukshuks served as guideposts to help travellers find their way across the otherwise featureless tundra.

Television

When television first came to the NWT in 1967, it was not used by northerners to communicate with other northerners. Virtually all programming came from the South. The television set, which was in almost every home, was rarely turned off. People liked the American shows so much that they began to lose interest in their own culture. This powerful threat to community interaction and Native culture still exists today, though perhaps to a lesser extent.

The Inuit Broadcasting Corporation started producing Inuit shows in 1981 and the Inuvialuit Communications Society in 1985,

Igloolik TV cameramen take shots of the town from an ice pan. For a long time, Igloolik residents would not allow TV in their community, regarding it as a threat to their culture. When they finally accepted it, they became leaders in the Inuit Broadcasting Corporation, and a lot of local programming is now created in Igloolik.

but these shows could only be seen once in a while. Regular airing of made-in-the-NWT programs didn't begin until 1983 with the CBC series "Focus North."

Then, in 1992, the Native peoples got their own television network. Called Television Northern Canada (TVNC), this network has 12 hours a day of original programming filmed and produced in the North, half of it in English or French, and half of it in aboriginal languages.

This is Canada's first broadcast network to be controlled totally by aboriginal people. It aims to serve an audience of 100 000 northerners scattered in 94 communities all the way from the Yukon to Nouveau Québec and Labrador. It has media centres in Whitehorse, Yellowknife and Iqaluit, and offers educational programs, news, entertainment, current affairs broadcasts and live phone-in shows. One cartoon show popular with kids features Super Shamou, an Inuit Superman. This truly northern channel is a powerful device for demonstrating and reinforcing traditional culture. However, it remains to be seen if it can compete with the still popular southern programs.

The Press

There are eight weekly newspapers and a number of community newsletters published in the NWT. *News/North* of Yellowknife has the highest circulation, at approximately 10 000. The highly regarded *Native Press* has a circulation of about 5000 in the western NWT, and in the east, the bilingual English-Inuktitut *Nunatsiaq News* of Iqaluit has a circulation of 3000.

Other newspapers are the *Drum* of Inuvik, the *Slave River Journal* of Fort Smith, the *Hub* of Hay River, the *Yellowknifer* and *L'Aquilon* of Yellowknife and the *Mackenzie Times* of Fort Simpson. Several magazines regularly publish stories of life on the last frontier: *Above and Beyond*, the award-winning *Up Here/Northwest Explorer* and *Arctic Circle*. Outcrop is the one resident publisher.

Below: The Inuvik Centennial Library displays artifacts as well as circulating books. *Right:* Library staff at the John Tsetso Memorial Library in Fort Simpson encourage young readers by providing a special "reading" teepee.

Libraries

Because the NWT has many small groups of people living vast distances apart, the NWT Public Library System, with headquarters in Hay River, moves books around from one community to another. One book may travel to half-a-dozen different communities in its lifetime, literally from one side of the continent to the other. Books may be written in any of the ten official languages. Videos, however, are the most popular of the circulated items; there are about 2700 of them.

Nineteen member libraries have buildings and a paid staff member, but books are also sent out to smaller communities to be placed in the care of somebody such as a teacher or an adult educator. Libraries in the NWT vary from a single room in a person's house to a comfortable, modern facility such as the one in a downtown Yellowknife shopping mall.

Telephones

The first two-way communication device in the NWT was not a telephone but a radio. By tuning their mobile, battery-operated systems to a particular frequency, people could contact each other in

Only about 20 percent of NWT communities are regularly accessible by road. The others, like Lac La Martre, are serviced mainly by air, and everyone turns out to meet the incoming planes that bring supplies, mail and visitors.

emergencies or just to catch up on the latest gossip. Even today, the Hunters' and Trappers' Channel on the Bush Radio allows people to keep in touch with each other while out on the land and far from a telephone.

Telephones have been a vital necessity in the NWT ever since the first one went into operation in Aklavik in 1925. People spend a lot of time on the phone. As of July 1992, the entire NWT was serviced by one company, NorthwesTel. There are about 30 000 phone lines, of which about 15 percent are business lines. The basic phone rental is the cheapest in Canada, but vast distances, remote locations, expensive repairs and the necessity for rare technologies mean that long-distance bills are high.

Postal Service

Mail service in the NWT varies from daily delivery, as in Yellowknife, to whenever someone happens to be going by, as at Lindberg Landing on the Liard Highway. Not all communities have post offices. Some, such as Colville Lake and Nahanni Butte, get their mail by courtesy bag service. This means that their mail is put in bags at the nearest post office and delivered by airplane. Then, someone in each community makes sure it gets distributed. As expected, the federal government subsidizes service to such areas.

CHAPTER TWELVE

Tourism: Within Reach Yet Beyond Belief

Many southerners mistakenly believe that the NWT is a land of endless cold, that it's barren and desolate, impossibly expensive and inaccessible, and that it's full of bugs.

The truth is that at times you can swim in the Arctic Ocean; that in places you can see kaleidoscopes of colourful flowers, herds of ten thousand caribou, and flocks of a million sea birds; and that if you're resourceful, there are ways to beat the cost of vast distances and mid-summer mosquitoes.

It's still an adventure to tour the NWT, but that's part of its appeal: adventures are fun. "Within Reach, Yet Beyond Belief" is how the Department of Tourism and Economic Development describes the vast country up here. The tourism industry is still small — only 30 000 people visited the NWT for pleasure in 1988 — but it's growing fast.

"Different" is perhaps the best word to describe the NWT's attractions. One tourist said that her summer vacation in the NWT was so different she felt she was not really in Canada. But one Canadian prime minister said you have not seen Canada until you've seen the North. Indeed, when the world thinks of Canada, it thinks of our North.

Back in the fifties and sixties, when northern tourism had just begun, only sportsfishermen and sportshunters went north. Now people come to raft a wild whitewater river, to kayak among the ice floes, to observe the birds, flowers and animals of the tundra, to see the northern lights or the midnight sun, to walk, ski, ride or fly to the North Pole.

Hiker on the bank of the Mountain River in the Mackenzie Mountains

They may come for these things, but it's likely they will go home talking about other things: watching an Inuk carve a soapstone walrus or a Métis make beaded moccasins, chatting with a Dene trapper, sharing smiles with an Inuit baby in her mother's *amouti* (woman's parka), sharing tea and *muktuk* or just meeting the friendly, open people of all the North's cultures. One Inuit outfitter says his clients come up "just to taste my bannock." In fact the Inuktitut word for "tourism" actually means "taking tea with a visitor."

The NWT is divided into eight travel zones from west to east: Northern Frontier, Big River, Nahanni-Ram, Sahtu, Delta-Beaufort, Arctic Coast, Keewatin and Baffin. Let's take a quick trip around this vast territory to see some of its highlights.

Northern Frontier

Yellowknife, on the north shore of Great Slave Lake, is the gateway to the Northern Frontier; for many travellers it's the gateway to the whole territory. As the capital city, it functions as the centre for administration, transportation and communication for both the east and west, although when the NWT is divided, Nunavut will have its own capital.

Yellowknife is a fascinating mix of the old and new, the funky and sedate. Elegant skyscrapers and innovative houses vie for space

The Yellowknife skyline reflected in the calm waters of Yellowknife Bay, on the North Arm of Great Slave Lake

beside prospectors' shacks and quonset huts, remnants left from the thirties when miners streamed into this wilderness to set up makeshift homes on a rock.

A unique walking trail winds around a downtown lake, meanders through stubby, Subarctic trees, and crosses some of the oldest rocks in the world. Yet it also nudges some fancy new buildings: the Visitors' Centre, the Legislative Assembly, the Prince of Wales Northern Heritage Centre, the iceberg-like Explorer Hotel and the aluminum Courthouse nicknamed the Giant Tin Can.

The people in Yellowknife are friendly, adaptable, imaginative and eccentric. They have a sense of fun: you can see that in the design of their buildings and the impossible places they put them. One house, a brown eraser-shaped box, seems to slide up a near-perpendicular cliff. Another is squeezed between a cliff and a bend in the road. Someone even made a home inside the first airplane to land at the North Pole.

There are any number of interesting places you can go from Yellowknife. Drive the Ingraham Trail, sail Great Slave Lake or cruise the Mackenzie River. Visit the nearby Dene communities that grew from fishing camps or trading posts: Detah, Rae-Edzo, Lac La Martre, Rae Lakes and Snare Lakes. Farther afield are dozens of lodges that can take you fishing, hunting, bird watching, caribou viewing, canoeing or dog sledding.

Above: **Sunset at Prelude Lake, on the Ingraham Trail.** *Left:* **Famous architect Gino Pin's house starts at the bottom of the cliff and slides uphill to the top, where it opens onto a garden and rock pool.**

Big River

The most popular way to enter the NWT is to drive up from Alberta on the Mackenzie Highway. This is called the Waterfalls Route because of the number of scenic waterfalls along the way.

Fort Smith, the Garden Capital of the North, is the headquarters for Wood Buffalo National Park, which is the second largest national park in the world and a World Heritage Site. It is also the entry point for the historic rapids and portage route on the Slave River, which attracts rafters from around the world.

Three tiny communities on the southern shores of Great Slave Lake are well worth visiting: Fort Resolution, a trading post built in 1786, the site of an important Roman Catholic school and hospital, and probably the oldest community in the NWT; Fort Reliance, where the explorers Back and Franklin wintered in 1821-22 (the remains of their winter house are still visible); and Snowdrift, or as it's now called, Lutselk'e.

Below: **Lady Evelyn Falls, on the Hay River.** *Right:* **The church at Fort Providence, a Dene community on the Mackenzie that began as a Catholic mission and developed as a Hudson's Bay Company post.** *Bottom right:* **They call it "the buffalo creep," a popular visitor activity at Wood Buffalo National Park.**

Near Hay River, the transportation hub of the western NWT, is the Hay River Dene Reserve, the only reserve in the territory. It was requested in 1974 by the Dene who wanted to protect their traditional lands and lifestyle.

Nahanni-Ram

"Rivers of Myth, Mountains of Mystery" are appropriate catchwords for this secret land between the Mackenzie Mountains and the Mackenzie River. Names on the map echo the legends and show why this land lures people from around the world: Headless Valley, Broken Skull River, Hell's Gate, Crash Lake, Death Canyon. They tell of mysterious mountain men, tropical valleys, gold prospectors and fur trappers who disappeared, and bush pilots whose planes crashed in forbidding terrain. They speak of landscapes that some say are more varied and spectacular than any in North America.

Left: The steep canyon walls of Ram Plateau are a favourite habitat of Dall's sheep. *Below:* Wind and weather have carved the soft sandstone rock of Nahanni National Park into fantastic shapes.

As it wends its way up and down the Mackenzie, the cruise ship *Norweta* stops now and again to allow visitors to explore the communities along the river banks.

The South Nahanni River, with its dramatic canyons, turbulent rivers, limestone mounds and hotsprings, traverses Nahanni National Park and World Heritage Site. The Ram Canyons are a maze of contorted gorges, honeycombed caves, rock bridges and sinkholes.

Fort Simpson, the oldest continuously occupied trading post on the Mackenzie River, is noted for its Papal Site, which commemorates the two visits in 1984 and 1987 of Pope John Paul II. Its key location on an island where the Liard and Mackenzie rivers meet and its accessibility by road make it a convenient jumping-off spot for exploring Nahanni-Ram country. Paddlers come to travel the Nahanni and Mackenzie rivers. Others come to explore the still largely traditional villages in the vicinity: Fort Liard, Nahanni Butte, Jean Marie, Trout Lake and Wrigley.

Sahtu

The Sahtu region stretches from the Mackenzie Mountains on the Yukon border across the Mackenzie River to Great Bear Lake. Sahtu is the Dene name for Great Bear Lake, which holds world records for trophy-size lake trout and arctic grayling. Nearby Tree River holds the record for arctic char.

A unique experience in Sahtu country is the Canol Heritage Trail, a National Historic Site that winds through a variety of landscapes. In this area you can see grizzlies, caribou, Dall's sheep, wolverines,

Left: **Just north of Fort Good Hope, the Mackenzie narrows into a canyon, the walls of which, known as the Ramparts, tower up to 80 metres (270 feet) over the river.**
Bottom left: **In true northern spirit, an Anglican and Roman Catholic church share the same building in Norman Wells.**
Bottom right: **One of the many brightly coloured frescoes in the Catholic mission church at Fort Good Hope**

marmots and several bird species that normally breed farther north.

Another National Historic Site is the Roman Catholic Church in Fort Good Hope, constructed in the 1860s and decorated by Father Petitot with ornate medieval-looking frescoes. Nearby Colville Lake is the last all-log community in the NWT.

Delta-Beaufort

There are two good ways to get to the Mackenzie Delta and the Beaufort Sea; cruise down the Mackenzie River or drive the Dempster Highway from the Yukon side.

The Dempster is the northernmost highway in North America. Its dramatic roller-coaster route climbs out of the trees near Dawson City, Yukon, crosses the stark tundra of the Eagle Plains at the Arctic Circle, rolls through the Richardson Mountains and then descends to the lowlands of the Peel and Mackenzie rivers. It passes the fishing and fur-trading communities of Arctic Red River and Fort

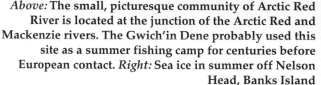

Above: The small, picturesque community of Arctic Red River is located at the junction of the Arctic Red and Mackenzie rivers. The Gwich'in Dene probably used this site as a summer fishing camp for centuries before European contact. *Right:* Sea ice in summer off Nelson Head, Banks Island

McPherson and ends after 743 kilometres (462 miles) in Inuvik. In winter an ice road continues over the frozen Beaufort Sea to Tuktoyaktuk.

Inuvik, the largest Canadian community north of the Arctic Circle, was planned as the NWT's first modern town. The government built it in 1961 to replace Aklavik, which seemed to be sinking into the Delta. But many Aklavik residents refused to leave their community and their rich muskrat-trapping grounds, so Aklavik became known as "The Town that Wouldn't Die." People also know Inuvik as "The Place of Man" because several cultures meet here: non-Native, Inuvialuit and Dene-Métis.

But Inuvik is not a destination; it is just a beginning. From here you can explore the highlights of the Mackenzie Delta and Beaufort Sea. Tuktoyaktuk has phenomenal pingos, exciting beluga whale hunts, artificial islands for oil and gas drilling and, right among the houses in the main street, the restored Roman Catholic mission schooner, *Our Lady of Lourdes.*

Sachs Harbour on Banks Island is one of the wealthiest communities in the North American Arctic because of its ambitious people and its rich white-fox trapping areas. Northern Banks Island has herds of musk-oxen, throngs of nesting snow geese and a number of the threatened Peary caribou.

One of Inuvik's claims to fame is the imaginative diversity of its buildings. Seen here, *clockwise from top left* are the "igloo" church, the ultra-modern Inuit Development Corporation headquarters, and a row of colourful apartment buildings known as Easter Egg Town.

Arctic Coast

Canada's "other coast" is the most sparsely populated region in the NWT and the one least visited today. Yet for five centuries, the whole world was intrigued with the elusive, fabled Northwest Passage. The real discoverers of the Northwest Passage, of course, were the ancestors of the Inuit who live today in eight small communities dotted along the convoluted coastline — Coppermine, Holman, Cambridge Bay, Umingmaktok, Bathurst Inlet, Gjoa Haven, Taloyoak (Spence Bay), Pelly Bay — and scattered outpost camps.

In contrast to the grim conditions suffered by both early Inuit and European explorers, today's travellers can experience the Northwest Passage in comfort by jet or luxury cruise ship.

In Gjoa Haven, where Roald Amundsen spent two winters, the story of the Inuit and the early explorers is told on cairns along a walking trail through the hamlet. Gjoa Haven is located on King William Island near the place where the only document of Franklin's last expedition was found. In Cambridge Bay, you can actually see the wreck of one of Amundsen's ships, the *Maud*. At Bathurst Inlet

Lodge, you can visit several of the places where Franklin camped during his gruelling 1821 expedition.

The Arctic coast offers tourists more than a history of the Northwest Passage, however. Other highlights are fishing and hiking along the Coppermine River, golfing at Holman on Victoria Island, seeing the stone churches built by the Oblate missionaries in Cambridge and Pelly Bay and watching Inuit at work in Taloyoak.

But the ultimate destination in this region is Bathurst Inlet Lodge, the only place in the NWT where you can see a typical Hudson's Bay Company trading post almost as it was in the heyday of the fur trade: the red-roofed company buildings, the pebble walkways, the mission church, the graveyard of Natives who died in the devastating epidemics brought on by European disease.

Bathurst Inlet, a true Arctic oasis, offers everything a visitor might want from a trip to the NWT. Of special significance is Nadlok, or "the crossing place," a Thule site on the Burnside River where houses were constructed from thousands of caribou antlers.

Keewatin

The Keewatin stretches from the Barren Lands to the west coast of Hudson Bay. Its one inland community, Baker Lake, is nicknamed the

Below: Caribou on the move in the Bathurst Inlet area. *Right:* Sailboats at Gjoa Haven, awaiting breakup to "do" the Northwest Passage

Belly Button of Canada because of its location at Canada's geographic centre.

The Keewatin calls itself the Accessible Arctic because visitors can have a genuine Arctic experience without travelling too far. Above the tree line, this area has spectacular wildlife scenes, including the half-million nesting snow geese at the McConnell River Bird Sanctuary; huge herds of migrating caribou and smaller herds of musk-oxen in the Thelon Game Sanctuary; thousands of nesting seabirds near Coats Island; and dozens of polar bears, pods of walrus and schools of beluga whales along the Hudson Bay coast. The proud, independent Inuit of the Keewatin, among the last Inuit to be lured into settlements, are now striving to keep their traditional culture alive.

From Rankin Inlet, the administrative centre of the region, you can fly to other Keewatin communities, such as Arviat, Coral Harbour and the nearby peninsula of Native Point, and Baker Lake.

Ijiraliq Archeological Site on the Meliadine River, where Inuit have camped for a thousand years, is perhaps the richest

Top left: **Legendary Marble Island, just off the west coast of Hudson Bay, near Rankin Inlet.** *Left:* **Inuit drum dancers perform at Baker Lake.** *Above:* **Ancient circle of stones at the Meliadine River archeological site near Rankin Inlet**

archeological site in the NWT. American and British whalers often stayed the winter at Marble Island, and you can still see their graves and the wrecks of their ships. Inuit custom requires that all visitors to Marble Island fall on their knees and crawl to shore as a sign of respect to the spirits of the many who died here, Inuit and non-Natives alike.

Baffin

Baffin, the largest zone in the NWT, stretches from Hudson Bay to the North Pole and includes Baffin Island, most of the High Arctic Islands and the Belcher Islands in James Bay. With spectacular ice fields, fiords, glaciers and icebergs, this is the Arctic of most people's imagination.

Its dramatic landscapes are best illustrated in Auyuittuq National Park, on Baffin Island and Ellesmere Island National Park Reserve. In any season, a flight along these coastlines is unforgettable.

Wilderness enthusiasts come to Pangnirtung from all over the world to hike Pangnirtung Pass in Auyuittuq and to climb the pristine peaks and glaciers that surround it. Ellesmere Island is hard to reach and much more expensive, but kayaking among the ice floes and hiking between Tanqueray Fiord and the thermal oasis of Lake Hazen attract the stout-hearted.

Kekerten Historic Park near Pangnirtung brings to life the whaling days of the nineteenth century, and in Qaummaarviit Historic Park near Iqaluit, visitors walk along boardwalks past remains of Thule Inuit life.

Apart from stunning scenery, the Baffin region has 14 intriguing communities conveniently linked by scheduled air service from Iqaluit, formerly called Frobisher Bay. In Pangnirtung, Clyde River and Cape Dorset, you can view magnificent works of art and then talk to the actual master artists who made them.

Igloolik and Hall Beach are noteworthy for their many archeological sites that date back 4000 years and for their custom of

Left: Hikers are dwarfed by the towering peak of Mt. Asgard in Auyuittuq National Park. *Above left:* Iqaluit, a town of about 3000 people, is the service and government centre for the Baffin region. *Above right:* Lake Harbour, considered by many to be the NWT's prettiest community

storing igoonuk, or fermented raw whale and walrus meat, in sausage-shaped bags of walrus hide under gravel mounds on the beach.

Backdropped by high hills, towering mountains and dramatic glaciers, Lake Harbour, Arctic Bay and Canada's northernmost community, Grise Fiord, vie with one another as the most photogenic communities in the NWT.

Off the beaten track is Sanikiluaq in the Belcher Islands, known for its distinctive soapstone carvings. Resolute, in contrast, is a bustling jumping-off point for scientists studying the High Arctic and an important base for trips to Ellesmere Island National Park Reserve and the magnetic and geographic North Poles.

Queen Elizabeth I dubbed Baffin *Meta Incognita,* the Edge of the Unknown. The tortuous terrain, which makes Baffin uniquely beautiful, will always keep parts of it unknown. There is a certain mystique in going to the uttermost ends of the Earth, not only for early Arctic explorers but for modern travellers as well. Each spring, a few adventurous tourists seeking the ultimate destination fly to Lake Hazen on Ellesmere Island to wait and see if the weather will allow their plane to land at the geographic North Pole.

Truly, the Northwest Territories is Canada's — and the world's — last frontier.

Facts
at a Glance

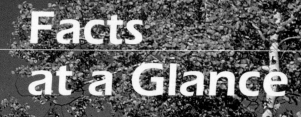

General Information

Entered Confederation: July 15, 1870

Territorial Capital: Yellowknife

Nicknames: Canada's Last Frontier, Land of the Polar Bear, North of Sixty

Territorial Flag: The blue panels at either side of the flag represent the lakes and waters of the Northwest Territories. The white centre panel symbolizes the ice and snow.

Territorial Coat of Arms: Two gold narwhals on the crest guard a compass rose, symbolic of the magnetic North Pole. The white upper third of the shield represents the polar ice pack, crossed by a wavy blue line portraying the Northwest Passage. The tree line separates green, symbolizing the forest, from red, symbolizing the Barren Lands. Gold ingots and the mask of a white fox represent commerce.

Territorial Flower: Mountain avens

Territorial Bird: Gyrfalcon

Territorial Tree: Jack pine

People

Population: 57 649 (1991 census)

Population Density: 1 person per 58.6 km² (22.6 per sq. mi.)

Population Distribution (by region)
(1991 census)

Fort Smith	47.8%
Baffin	19.7%
Inuvik	14.7%
Keewatin	10.1%
Kitikmeot	7.6%

Population Growth

1911	6 507
1931	9 316
1951	16 004
1961	22 998
1971	34 804
1981	45 741
1991	57 649

Ethnic Composition of Population
(1991 census)

Non-Native	22 347 (38.8%)
Inuit	21 565 (37.4%)
Dene	9 647 (16.7%)
Métis	4 090 (7.1%)

Languages: There are ten official languages: English, Inuktitut (two dialects), Slavey (two dialects), Dogrib, Chipewyan, Gwich'in, Cree and French.

Largest communities: Yellowknife (15 179), Iqaluit (3552), Hay River (3206), Inuvik (3206)
(1991 census)

Geography

Total Area: 3 376 689 km² (1 303 842 sq. mi.), 34% of Canada

Freshwater Area: 133 294 km² (51 467 sq. mi.), 20% of Canada's freshwater

Greatest Distance: From east to west, 3283 km (2040 mi.), Baffin Island to Yukon border; from south to north, James Bay to Ellesmere Island, 3404 km (2115 mi.)

Coastline: 30 000 km (19 000 mi.), 24% of Canada's coastline

Highest Point: Unnamed peak in the Mackenzie Mountains, 2762 m (9062 ft.), and Mt. Barbeau on Ellesmere Island, 2616 m (8583 ft.)

Borders: The NWT is bordered by the Yukon on the west and, by British Columbia, Alberta, Saskatchewan and Manitoba on the south.

Glaciers: Baffin has 10 526 glaciers covering 35 890 km² (13 858 sq. mi.); Ellesmere Island has an unknown number of glaciers covering 77 596 km² (29 962 sq. mi.); Axel Heiberg Island has 1121 glaciers covering 11 383 km² (4395 sq. mi.).

Rivers: The main rivers are the Mackenzie with its chief tributaries, Trout, Willowlake, Root, North Nahanni, Keele, Great Bear, Mountain and Arctic Red; the Liard with its tributaries, South Nahanni and Petitot; the long winding rivers that cross the Barren Lands to flow north to the Arctic Ocean, Anderson, Hornaday, Coppermine, Hood, Burnside, Western, Ellice and Back; the Thelon, which flows east across the Barren Lands to Baker Lake and eventually to Hudson Bay. There are many, many more.

Lakes: There are countless lakes in the NWT, the biggest being Great Bear Lake (31 400 km²/12 100 sq. mi., the fourth largest in North America), Great Slave Lake (28 438 km²/10 980 sq. mi., the fifth largest in North America). Other sizeable lakes include Nettling Lake, Amadjuak Lake, Dubawnt Lake and Baker Lake.

Topography: The NWT has four main physiographic regions: the Precambrian or Canadian Shield, the Plains or Lowlands, the Innuitian and the Cordilleran.

The Precambrian Shield occupies over half of the NWT, including part of the Arctic Islands. It begins north of Great Bear Lake and follows the tree line southeast into the North Arm of Great Slave Lake and the provinces. It is characterized by many lakes, patches of muskeg and rock outcrops.

The Plains are formed on what was

Lichen-covered erratics — boulders scattered by the glaciers of the last ice age

once an inland sea. This area may be divided into the Western Plains, the Arctic Lowlands, the Arctic Coastal Plain and the Hudson Bay Lowland. Below the tree line, the land is bush with thick soil. Above the tree line, it is sparsely vegetated, lake-dotted tundra.

The Innuitian region lies entirely within a huge triangle of islands called the Arctic Archipelago. The islands are part of a great plateau that slopes upwards to high mountains on its eastern edge. Permanent ice sheets cover most of the eastern Arctic Islands.

The Cordilleran region is part of the same great mountain barrier that extends down the western part of the continent. The Mackenzie, Selwyn, Richardson and Franklin mountains range from 900 to over 2700 m (3000 to 9000 ft.) in altitude.

Climate: There are two types of climate — Arctic and Subarctic. The Arctic lies above the tree line. Wind, lack of moisture, permafrost and a thin layer of soil prevent trees from growing. On average, the total snowfall a year is only 78 cm (31 in.). In Resolute, the mean January temperature is -32°C (-25.6°F). The average south Baffin Island high in July is 10°C (50°F), with an occasional reading as high as 24°C (75°F). The frost-free period in inhabited areas ranges from 40 to 60 days.

The Subarctic lies below the tree line. Summers are warm, sometimes hot. The average July high is 21°C (70°F). The mean temperature in January is -28.6°C (-19°F), and the average snowfall is 119 cm (47 in.) a year. The frost-free period depends on nearness to water; it ranges from 50 to 100 days.

Nature

Vegetation: There may be no trees on the Arctic Tundra but at Arctic oases and during the brief weeks of summer, there can be dozens of lichens, ferns and mosses; shrubs such as willow, alder, birch, Labrador tea and Lapland rosebay; berries, including bearberry, crowberry, soapberry and blueberry; and a surprising multitude of showy plants such as orchids, moss campion, saxifrage, arctic poppy, mountain avens, arctic lupin, liquorice root, alpine azalea, fireweed, paintbrush, rock jasmine and the common dandelion.

Trees in the Subarctic Forest-Tundra and the Boreal Forest include tall willow, aspen, birch, jack pine, white and black spruce, tamarack and balsam poplar. There are many different kinds of berry plants such as juniper, Saskatoon, cranberry, raspberry, strawberry and blueberry. Flowers include wild rose, twin-flower, wintergreen, cinquefoil, fireweed and dwarf dogwood.

Fish: There are fewer varieties of fish in the NWT than in the South. Principal species include polar cod, grayling, walleye (pickerel), great northern pike, arctic char, dolly varden, lake trout, whitefish.

Reptiles and Amphibians: Only one species of reptile (the garter snake) and five amphibians (wood frog, chorus frog, leopard frog, Canadian toad, and Hudson Bay Toad) inhabit the NWT.

Marine Mammals: Ringed, harp, bearded and hooded seals; walrus; bowhead, finback, humpback, beluga and killer whales; harbour porpoise; narwhal.

Land Mammals: Small mammals such as shrew, bat, pika, snowshoe and arctic hare, arctic ground squirrel (commonly called siksik), red squirrel, porcupine, mice, voles and lemming; furbearers such as wolf, arctic fox, muskrat, marten, mink, wolverine, beaver and lynx; big game such as grizzly and polar bears, caribou, moose, wood bison, musk-ox, mountain goat and Dall's sheep.

Birds: Most of the birds found in the NWT are migratory summer residents. These include one-fifth of the continental population of ducks, geese and swans, as well as the world populations of greater snow geese, Atlantic brant and Ross's geese. Birds that reside here all year are the snowy owl, rock ptarmigan, gyrfalcon and raven. Others that frequent the forest, the tundra and the sea coast are too numerous to name.

National Parks and Park Reserves: Aulavik, Auyuittuq, Ellesmere, Nahanni, Wood Buffalo — 60% of Canada's National Park Area

Some Territorial Parks: Blackstone, Qaummaarviit, Kekerten, Saamba Deh, Fred Henne, Northwest Passage

Game Sanctuaries: Thelon (largest), Dewey Soper, Bowman Bay, Mackenzie Bison (and Peel River Preserve and Reindeer Grazing Reserve)

Bird Sanctuaries: Queen Maud Gulf (largest), Bylot Island, Kendall Island, Anderson River Delta, Banks Island, McConnell River, Harry Gibbons, East Bay, Cape Dorset

Minerals: Uranium, tungsten, lead-zinc, copper, silver, gold, rare metals, barite, diamonds, coal, oil and gas are among the most plentiful.

Government

Federal: The NWT has two seats in the House of Commons, one from the Western Arctic and one from the Eastern Arctic, and one Senate seat.

Territorial: A commissioner appointed by the federal government is chief executive officer of the NWT. This role is similar to that of a lieutenant-governor in provincial jurisdictions. The NWT is governed by a legislative assembly of 24 elected members. An executive council or cabinet is chosen from its members, as is the head of the assembly, known as the government leader. There are no political parties in the legislative assembly.

Local: The government of the NWT has five administrative regions: Baffin, Fort Smith, Inuvik, Keewatin and Kitikmeot. Some communities within the regions are administered by municipal councils, some by band councils and some by territorial regional offices.

Education

The GNWT Department of Education in Yellowknife works with eleven local boards to provide education for about 15 000 students in 83 schools. Most communities now have schools and teach kindergarten to grade 9.

Students from small communities are flown to larger communities to attend high school. They live in residences or boarding homes. Generous funding is given to students who wish to study at college or university. About 20 grade 10 to 12 students from the western part of the NWT who show academic excellence and a potential for leadership are enrolled in a special two-year leadership program in Fort Smith.

Educators are working hard to make schools meet the specific needs of their students. For instance, they offer flexible timetables for those who wish to hunt, trap and fish with their families; bilingual instruction at least to grade 3 (the local Native language as well as English); Native teachers and classroom assistants; locally produced learning materials; and a compulsory Northern Studies course.

Nevertheless, many Native students drop out of school; over half the Native people of working age do not finish grade 10, and few choose to finish grade 12.

Arctic College is the only post secondary educational institution. It has six campuses and more than 30 community learning centres. Arctic College tries to help adult northerners in such things as the three Rs, job training, northern studies and preparing for university.

Arctic College, Inuvik

Economy and Industry

Value of Industries: (1992)

Oil and Gas: $261.1 million

Tourism: $88.8 million. NWT's most rapidly growing industry.

Subsistence Economy: $54 million

Arts and Crafts: $22.5 million

Sports Fishing: $16.2 million

Sports Hunting: $8.4 million

Commercial Fishing: $3.4 million

Fur Production: $2.8 million

Agriculture: $1.8 million

Canoes from villages along the Mackenzie River hold a race to commemorate Alexander Mackenzie's 1789 journey down the river.

Forestry: The GNWT has set a target for increasing forestry production by 1995 to bring in about $6.5 million annually.

Cost of living: It costs a lot more to live up North than it does down South, largely because of higher transportation and heating costs, and lack of competition. And the farther north you live, the more expensive it is, as a small sampling of food costs in Yellowknife (A) and Pelly Bay (B) in early 1993 shows:

	A	B
1 L (qt.) milk	$1.21	$3.99
454 gm (16oz.) loaf of bread	1.66	3.49
1 kg (2.2lb.) ground meat	6.20	9.44
can of pop	0.91	2.50

Important Dates

Thousands of years before specific dates can be assigned to events, the ancestors of the Dene and the Inuit had established themselves in the lands now known as the Northwest Territories.

1000	Norsemen visit Baffin Island.
1576-78	Martin Frobisher makes three voyages to Baffin Island.
1670	Hudson's Bay Company is formed.
1769-72	Samuel Hearne of the HBC explores the Barren Lands.
1789	Alexander Mackenzie explores the river that now bears his name.
1819-23	William Edward Parry explores the Arctic Islands.
1837-39	Thomas Simpson and Peter Warren Dease of the HBC survey the Arctic coastline.
1845-48	Sir John Franklin and his crew perish while their ships are frozen for two winters in Victoria Strait.
1850-54	Robert McClure discovers McClure Strait between Banks and Melville islands.
1870	Canada acquires HBC lands; a tiny province of Manitoba is created, and the rest becomes known as the North-West Territories.
1880	The British government turns over the Arctic Archipelago to the Dominion of Canada.
1898	The Yukon Territory is created.

1899	Dene sign Treaty 8.
1903-6	Roald Amundsen in the *Gjoa* makes the first sea crossing of the complete Northwest Passage.
1905	The provinces of Saskatchewan and Alberta are carved out of the North-West Territories.
1908-9	Robert Peary claims to have reached the North Pole.
1908-12	Vilhjalmur Stefansson explores the western part of the North-West Territories.
1912	The NWT acquires its present-day boundaries.
1919	Dene sign Treaty 11.
1921	Oil is discovered near Norman Wells.
1930	Pitchblende is discovered on Great Bear Lake.
1933	Gold is discovered in Yellowknife Bay.
1942	Construction begins on the Canol Highway and Pipeline.
1950s	The Distant Early Warning (DEW) Line and an all-weather Mackenzie Highway are constructed.
1960s	Inuit arts-and-crafts industry expanded and a co-operative movement established.
1967	Yellowknife becomes capital of the NWT and site of a resident government.
1969	Indian Brotherhood formed.
1970	First Northern Games held.
1972	Métis Association established.
1974	Dene Declaration requests self-determination.

1975	GNWT Territorial Council fully elected.
1977	Berger Report recommends 10-year postponement of Mackenzie Valley Pipeline.
1978	Dene Nation proclaimed.
1979	Dempster Highway opens.
1981	Existing aboriginal and treaty rights recognized in the Canadian Constitution.
1982	A plebiscite says yes to dividing the NWT.
1983	Liard Highway opens; Richard Nerysoo is the first Native to be chosen as government leader.
1984	Inuvialuit of COPE have their land claims approved.
1985	Canada and the United States agree to develop a new radar line, the North Warning System.
1989	Dan Norris becomes first Native commissioner.
1991	Tungavuk Federation of Nunavut (TFN) signs an agreement-in-principle to settle their land claims.
1992	Nellie Cournoyea becomes government leader, the first woman head of government in Canada.
1992	Plebiscite confirms division of the NWT into two territories.
1993	Federal government and Inuit representatives sign the Tungavik Nunavut land claim settlement; Parliament ratifies the settlement and passes legislation to create the new territory of Nunavut.

John Amagoalik

Ethel Blondin-Andrew

George Blondin

Tom Butters

Some Noteworthy People

Many people from many countries and several cultures have contributed to the Northwest Territories — people who have always lived there, people who came for a time and left a permanent mark and people who have just begun to make their mark. What follows is only a tiny sample.

John Amagoalik (1947 -), born on the land near Inoudjouac (Port Harrison), grew up in Resolute, vocal supporter of a tree line boundary to divide the NWT; past president and director of land claims for the Inuit Tapirisat of Canada (ITC); longtime member of the Tungavik Federation of Nunavut

Caroline Anawak (1948 -), came north in 1969; consultant, teacher; cross-cultural specialist; married Dene leader James Wah-shee and helped to organize the Indian Brotherhood (Dene Nation); later married Inuit leader Jack Anawak; actively involved in tourism and social work

Jack Anawak (1959 -), born and raised on the land near Repulse Bay; hunter and trapper but also active in business and politics; held executive positions in several Inuit organizations; was mayor of Rankin Inlet and has been Liberal MP for the Eastern Arctic since 1988

John Anderson-Thomson (1900 - 1985), came to Yellowknife in 1944; outstanding engineer, geologist and pioneer Arctic surveyor, also longtime justice of the peace and police magistrate

Stephen Angulalik (1895 - 1980), born on the land near Queen Maud Gulf; renowned leader, hunter, trapper, trader, carver, photographer, storyteller and record keeper; one of the few Natives to work as an independent trader in the NWT

Beck Family, Métis sled dog racers; Ray Beck pioneered the sport in the 1950s and 1960s; his sons Roger, Raymond Jr., Arthur and Eric are all dog sledders, as are his nephews Grant Beck Jr. and Richard Beck, who between them have won 7 Canadian and 2 World Championships

Thomas Berger (1933 -), lawyer, judge, writer, environmentalist; recommended Native land claims negotiations and a moratorium on a gas pipeline in the Yukon or the NWT until land claims are settled

Ethel Blondin-Andrew (1951 -), born in Fort Norman; teacher, language specialist, administrator, politician; Liberal MP for the Western Arctic since 1988; the first Native woman to be elected to Parliament in Canada

George Blondin (1922 -), born at Horton Lake; philosopher, statesman, columnist, chairman of the Denendeh Elders Council; has been a miner, hunter and trapper, chief of Fort Franklin and vice-president of Dene Nation; author of *When the World Was New*, a book on the history and legends of his people

William C. Bompas (1836 - 1906), Anglican missionary who spent 40 years in Northern Canada; first bishop of the vast Mackenzie River diocese; translated scripture and hymns into a number of Dene dialects

Tom Butters, born in Vancouver, resident in the North since 1947; administrator, businessman, politician, publisher of *The Drum*, a newspaper in Inuvik; in 1970 became the first elected MLA for the Western Arctic (Inuvik)

Nellie Cournoyea (1940 -), born at Aklavik; radio announcer, land rights worker and business administrator for the Committee for Original Peoples' Entitlement (COPE) and the ITC; MLA since 1979; elected government leader in 1992, the first woman head of government in Canada

Tagak Curley (1944 -), born in Coral Harbour; politician and administrator; founding member and first president of ITC; has been executive director of Inuit Cultural Institute, president of Nunasi Business Development

Corporation and an MLA and cabinet member for the GNWT

Punch Dickins (1899 -), bush pilot; made aviation history in 1923 by carrying the first airmail into the Canadian Arctic; developed the de Havilland Beaver, one the best Canadian bush planes; named Officer of the British Empire in 1936 and of the Order of Canada in 1968

Pinto Dragon (1971 -), Métis born in Fort Smith; hockey player; played centre for Cornell University in the United States while earning a degree in business administration and natural resource management; drafted to NHL Pittsburgh Penguins in 1992

Edna Elias (1956 -), born in a hunting camp west of Cambridge Bay; teacher, president of NWT Advisory Council on the Status of Women, director of the Language Bureau of the GNWT, first female mayor of Coppermine

Bob Engle (1922 -), founded Northwest Territorial Airways; pioneered many of the scheduled routes across the NWT, established Northwest International Airways Ltd.; member of Order of Canada for services to aviation

Georges Erasmus (1948 -), born in Fort Rae; politician and Native rights activist since 1973; president of the Indian

Nellie Cournoyea

Tagak Curley

Punch Dickins

Pinto Dragon

Georges Erasmus

Etuangat (Aksayook)

Shirley Firth

Ann Hanson

Brotherhood, negotiator for the Dene-Métis Land Claims Agreement-in-Principle, national chief of the Assembly of First Nations (AFN) 1985-91; member of Order of Canada

Etuangat (Aksayook) (1900 -), born near Pangnirtung; whaler, carver, storyteller; one of the last whalers whose memories bring life to the interpretation of historical parks such as Kekerten; respected elder who saved the lives of many people by bringing them by dogteam to the hospital in Pangnirtung

Shirley and Sharon Firth (1953 -), Métis twin sisters born and raised on a trapline in the Mackenzie Delta; pioneer cross-country skiers; between them they have won up to 100 medals in national competitions and were on the National Ski Team for 17 years; received Order of Canada in 1984

Father René Fumoleau (1926 -), Oblate missionary, outspoken champion of the Dene; filmmaker; wrote *As Long As This Land Shall Last*, the first history book about Native people of the North

Ann Meekitjuk Hanson, born near Lake Harbour; broadcaster, interpreter, translator; member of various scientific, education and health boards; a deputy commissioner of the NWT

Stuart Hodgson (1924 -), labour leader and government administrator; appointed to the NWT Council in 1962; deputy commissioner (1965-67), commissioner (1967-79); responsible for setting up the first government in Yellowknife

James Houston (1921-), government administrator, artist, novelist, filmmaker; introduced printmaking to the Inuit of Baffin Island and Inuit art to the world; most famous book and film is *The White Dawn*

Helen Kalvak (1901 - 1984), born near Holman Island; highly respected artist and printmaker; noted for her simple but powerful themes; member of the Order of Canada and the Royal Canadian Academy of Arts

Kenojuak (1927 -), born on the land at Ikirisaq; artist, sculptor and muralist; best known for "The Enchanted Owl," which was reproduced on a postage stamp in 1967; first Native to receive the Order of Canada (1967); member of the Royal Canadian Academy of Arts

Rosemary Kuptana (1953 -), born in Sachs Harbour; journalist, broadcaster, author, administrator, politician; as the first woman president of the Inuit Broadcasting Corporation, helped develop Native programming; became president of the ITC; received the Order of Canada in 1988

Henry Larsen (1899 - 1964), born in Norway; explorer, seaman and RCMP officer; patrolled Arctic waters for 12 years in *St. Roch*, first boat to sail through the Northwest Passage both ways (1940-42 and 1944)

Markoosie (1941 -), born in Northern Quebec, relocated to Resolute in 1953; first Inuk to become a qualified bush pilot; journalist and author of *Harpoon of the Hunter* and many short stories

Cece McCauley, Métis born in Fort Norman; businesswoman, politician, columnist and artist known for her appliquéd wall hangings; the first female Dene chief in the western NWT

Pat McMahon (1945 -), came to Yellowknife in 1968; businesswoman and tireless member of many local and national organizations; mayor since 1987, enthusiastic promoter of tourism

Richard Nerysoo, born near Fort McPherson; politician, land claims negotiator and vice-president of the Dene Nation; first Native to serve as government leader (1983-85)

Dan Norris (1935 -), born near Inuvik; senior administrator in territorial and federal governments; first northerner and Native commissioner of the NWT (1989)

Jessie Oonark (1906 - 1985), born in the Back River area; one of the finest and most original of all Inuit artists; made prints and wall hangings, including a commissioned wall hanging for the National Arts Centre in Ottawa; member of the Royal Canadian Academy of Arts

John Parker (1929 -), mining engineer, businessman, politician; mayor of Yellowknife (1963-67), deputy commissioner of the NWT (1967-79), commissioner (1979-1989); received the Order of Canada for guiding the evolution of municipal and territorial government

Émile Petitot (1838 - 1916), Roman Catholic missionary, mapmaker, linguist; travelled widely in the area of the Mackenzie, Anderson and Yukon rivers; developed several Dene dictionaries

Pitseolak Ashoona (1904-1983), born at Nottingham Island; one of the most famous Inuit artists whose drawings and prints have sold around the world; member of the Royal Canadian Academy of Arts and the Order of Canada

Peter Pitseolak (1906 - 1973), born near Cape Dorset; artist, photographer and respected leader; one of the first Inuit painters and photographers

Kenojuak

Cece McCauley

Richard Nerysoo

Dan Norris

Pitseolak Ashoona

Bertha Ruben

John R. Sperry

James Wah-shee

Bertha Ruben (1925 -), born on the land near Paulatuk; artist, well-respected mother of more than 20 children, including internationally known sculptors **Abraham Anghik** and **David Piqtoukun;** with her husband, **Billy Ruben,** also an artist, she has participated in all Northern Games since 1970

Terry Ryan (1933 -), awarded Order of Canada in 1985 for 25 years as general manager of the West Baffin Inuit Cooperative in Cape Dorset; carried on from James Houston in promoting and maintaining international reputation of Inuit art

Agnes Semmler (1910 -), Métis businesswoman, politician; co-founder and president of COPE; Woman of the Century representing the North (1967); deputy commissioner of the NWT (1984-87)

Jack Sissons (1892 - 1969), came to Yellowknife as the first judge of the NWT; made legal history by bringing justice to the people in the place where the offence occurred and basing his judgements on the Native point of view; nicknamed "Ekoktoegee" (the one who listens) by the Inuit

John R. Sperry (1924 -), Anglican missionary and third bishop of the Arctic; translated prayerbook, hymns and gospels into the Copper Inuit dialect

Isaac Stringer (1866-1934), born in England; Anglican missionary, served Dene, Inuvialuit and whalers; known as "The Bishop Who Ate His Boots" because he travelled extensively and suffered many hardships on the trail

Mona Thrasher (1942 -), Inuvialuk born in the Mackenzie Delta; unable to hear or speak but gifted with a unique artistic talent; paints realistic scenes of traditional life in oils and pastels that emphasize human activity; major works include the Stations of the Cross in the Igloo Church in Inuvik

John Tsetso (1921 - 1964), born in the bush near the Mackenzie River; trapper and writer; wrote the first book published by a Dene, *Trapping Is My Life*

James Wah-shee (1945 -), born in Fort Rae; community worker and politician; founding member and president of the Indian Brotherhood; land claims coordinatior for the Métis Association, MLA for the GNWT; now involved in business administration

Glenn Warner (1933 -), RCMP officer in NWT (1951-72); pilot, businessman, consultant; promoter of all aspects of the NWT, especially tourism and the environment; his wife, son and daughters are also actively involved in tourist and aviation industries

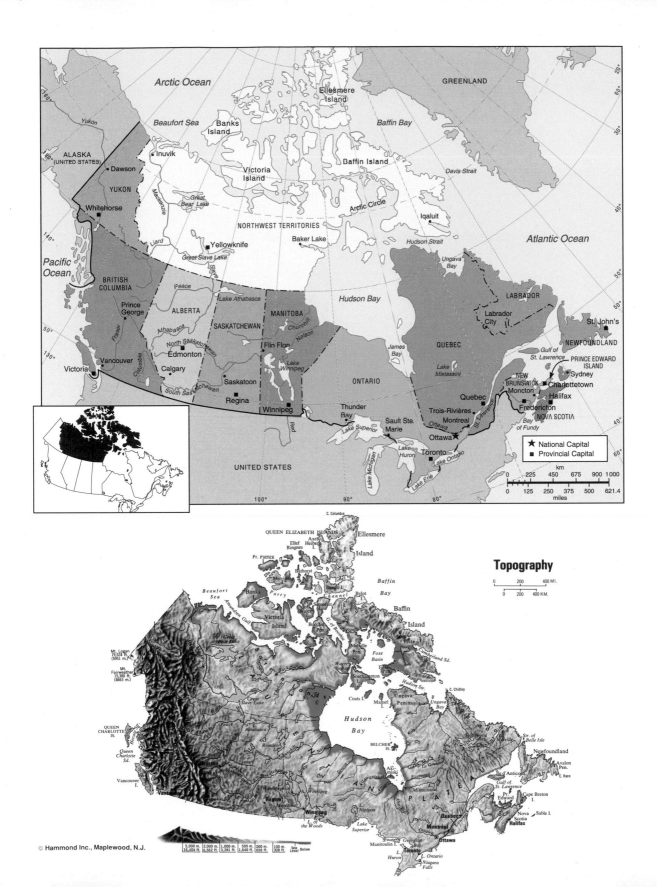

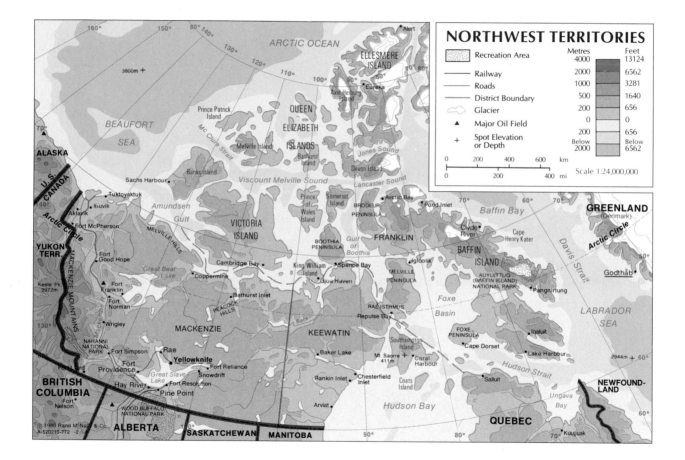

NORTHWEST TERRITORIES

		Metres	Feet
	Recreation Area	4000	13124
	Railway	2000	6562
	Roads	1000	3281
	District Boundary	500	1640
	Glacier	200	656
▲	Major Oil Field	0	0
+	Spot Elevation or Depth	200	656
		Below 2000	Below 6562

0   200   400   600   km
0   200   400   mi

Scale 1:24,000,000

ARCTIC OCEAN

ELLESMERE ISLAND

Alert

Eureka

Axel Heiberg Island

Prince Patrick Island

QUEEN ELIZABETH ISLANDS

3800m +

BEAUFORT SEA

Melville Island

Bathurst Island

Devon Island

Jones Sound

ALASKA

Banks Island

Sachs Harbour

Viscount Melville Sound

Lancaster Sound

Arctic Bay

Pond Inlet

Baffin Bay

GREENLAND
(Denmark)

U.S.
CANADA

Tuktoyaktuk

Inuvik

Aklavik

Fort McPherson

Arctic Circle

Amundsen Gulf

Mc Clure Strait

Prince of Wales Island

Somerset Island

BRODEUR PENINSULA

BOOTHIA PENINSULA

Clyde River

Cape Henry Kater

Arctic Circle

YUKON TERR.

Fort Good Hope

MELVILLE HILLS

VICTORIA ISLAND

FRANKLIN

BAFFIN ISLAND

Davis Strait

Godthåb

Keele Pk. 2972m

Fort Franklin

Great Bear Lake

Cambridge Bay

Coppermine

King William Island

Gulf of Boothia

Spence Bay

Igloolik

MELVILLE PENINSULA

AUYUITTUQ (BAFFIN ISLAND) NATIONAL PARK

Pangnirtung

LABRADOR SEA

Fort Norman

PEACOCK HILLS

Bathurst Inlet

Gjoa Haven

Back

RAE ISTHMUS

Foxe Basin

Wrigley

MACKENZIE

Repulse Bay

KEEWATIN

FOXE PENINSULA

Iqaluit

NAHANNI NATIONAL PARK

Fort Simpson

Rae

Yellowknife

Fort Reliance

Southampton Island

Mt. Saorre 411m

Coral Harbour

Cape Dorset

Lake Harbour

2944m +

Fort Liard

Fort Providence

Snowdrift

Fort Resolution

Great Slave Lake

Baker Lake

Chesterfield Inlet

Coats Island

Salluit

Hudson Strait

NEWFOUND-LAND

BRITISH COLUMBIA

Fort Nelson

Hay River

Pine Point

Rankin Inlet

Chesterfield Inlet

WOOD BUFFALO NATIONAL PARK

Arviat

Hudson Bay

Ungava Bay

© 1980 Rand M?Nally & Co.
A-520210-772 -2-

ALBERTA

SASKATCHEWAN

MANITOBA

QUEBEC

Kuujjuak

AVERAGE ANNUAL RAINFALL

Most of the Northwest Territories receives less than 15 inches—375 mm—of precipitation a year, much of it in the form of rain during the summer.

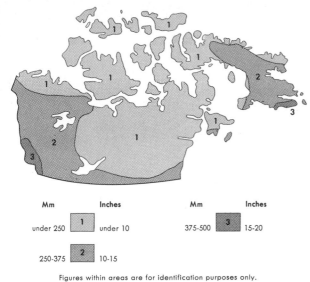

Mm		Inches	Mm		Inches
under 250	1	under 10	375-500	3	15-20
250-375	2	10-15			

Figures within areas are for identification purposes only.

GROWING SEASON

Most of the Northwest Territories has less than three frost-free months each year.

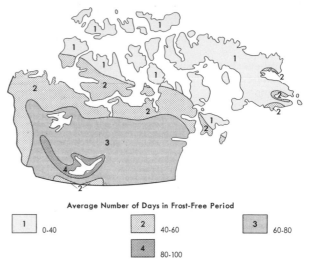

Average Number of Days in Frost-Free Period

1	0-40	2	40-60	3	60-80	
4	80-100					

Figures within areas are for identification purposes only.

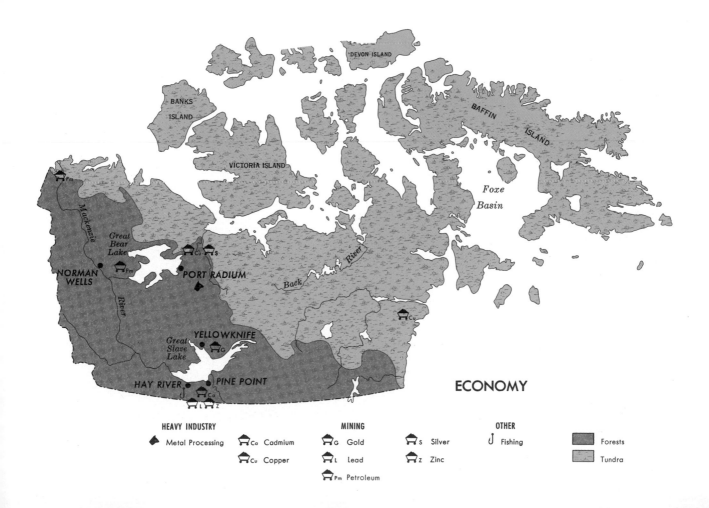

ECONOMY

HEAVY INDUSTRY
- Metal Processing

MINING
- Ca Cadmium
- Cu Copper
- Pm Petroleum
- G Gold
- L Lead
- S Silver
- Z Zinc

OTHER
- Fishing
- Forests
- Tundra

Index

Page numbers that appear in
boldface type indicate
illustrations

Adams, Willie, 62
Aglukark, Susan, 82
air service, 48, 51-52, 53
Akaitcho, 37, **38**
Aklavik, 104
Amagoalik, John, 118, **118**
Amundsen, Roald, 39, 105
Anawak, Caroline, 118
Anawak, John (Jack), 62, 118
Anderson-Thomson, John, 118
Anghik, Abraham, 122
Angulalik, Stephen, 118
animal life, 24-27, **25**, 73, 102-3,
    104, 107, 113-14
Arctic Circle, 19
Arctic Coast, 105-6
Arctic College, 115
Arctic Red River, 41, 103, **104**
Arctic Winter Games, 85, **86**
arts and crafts, 34, 58, 59, 77, 78-
    83, 89, 115
aurora borealis, **21**
Auyuittuq National Park, 108, **109**
Back, Sir George, 37
Baffin Island, **12**, 13, 31, 37, 58, 88,
    108
Baffin region, 62, 111
Baker Lake, 32, 81, 89, 106-7
Banks Island, 43, 104
Bathurst Inlet, 33, 105, 106
Beck Family, 118
Belcher Islands, 108, 109
Berger, Thomas, 118
Berger Report, 73
birds, 24, 25, 26-27, 107, 113-14
Blondin-Andrew, Ethel, 62, 118,
    118
Blondin, George, 88, **118**, 119
Blondin, John, 30, 83
Bompas, William C., 119
Bourque, Marvin, **34**
bush pilots, 48, 51-52
Butters, Tom, **118**, 119
Cambridge Bay, 55, **56**, 75, 105,
    106

Canadian Shield, 10-11
Canol Heritage Trail, 102-3
Cantung mine, 71
Cape Dorset, 31, 58, 81, 108
caribou, 24-25, 26, **106**
CBC North, 82, 91
churches, 44-45, 47-48, **100**, **103**
climate, 20-21, 113
commissioners, 61-62, 114
communication, 41, 90-95
Committee of Original Peoples'
    Entitlement, 64
conservation, 26-27
Cook, Frederick, 39, 40
co-operatives, 58-59
cost of living, 116
Cournoyea, Nellie, 62, **119**
Curley, Tagak, 119, **119**
defence installations, 52, 55, 91
Dempster, W.J., 48
Dempster Highway, **46**, 48, 53,
    103-4
Dene, 29-31, **30**, 43-44, 49, 64, 67,
    77, 79-80, 81, 82, 83, 85-86, 88,
    99, 101, 111
Dene Nation, 63
Denendeh, 9, 66-67
Dickins, Punch, 51, 119, **119**
Diefenbaker, John, 53
diseases, 44, 56
Distant Early Warning Line, 55
division, 66-67
Dorset culture, 31-32
Dragon, Pinto, 119, **119**
drum dances, 82, 83, **107**
economy, 55, 58-59, 66, 68-77,
    115-16
education, 45, 65, 115
elections, 64
Elias, Edna, 119
Ellesmere Island, 108
Engle, Bob, 119
English Chief, 41
environmental concerns, 26-27
Erasmus, Georges, 119-20, **120**
Etuangat (Aksayook), 120, **120**
farming, **76**, 77, 115
festivals, 85-87
Firth, Shirley and Sharon, 120, **120**

fish species, 24, 26, 113
fishing, 31, 33, 69, 75, 102, 115
forests, 22, 75, **76**, 113, 116
Fort Good Hope, 41, 65, 103
Fort Liard, 29, 41, 81
Fort McPherson, 41, 47, 48, 104
Fort Providence, 81, 100
Fort Resolution, **40**, 41, 100
Fort Simpson, 49, 53, 77, 94, 102
Fort Smith, 35, 49, 62, 77, 100, 111
Franklin, John, 35, 38
Fumoleau, René, 120
fur trade, 34, 40-42, 43, 73, 115
geography, 7-20, 112-13
Gjoa Haven, 105, **106**
glaciers, 12-13, 16, 112
government, 35, 47-51, 56-57, 60-
    67, 114
Great Bear Lake, 15, 75, 102
Great Slave Lake, 15, 22, 75
Green, Jim, 82
Grise Fiord, 56, 109
Hall Beach, **54**, 55, 108
Hanson, Ann Meekitjuk, 120, **120**
Hay River, 35, 77, 94, 101, 111
Hearne, Samuel, **40**, 41
Herschel Island, 43, 47
historical dates, 116-17
Hodgson, Stuart, 61, 120
Holman, 81, 105, 106
housing, **16**, 56-57
Houston, James, 58, 120
Hudson's Bay Company, 40-41,
    43, 106
Hunters' and Trappers' channel,
    91, 95
hunting, 26, 31, 33, 69, 73-75, 115
ice formations, 12, 13, 15, 16, 17,
    37, 104
ice roads, 53, 70, 71, 104
Igloolik, **59**, 88, 92, 108
Ijiraliq Archeological Site, **107**,
    107-8
Ingraham Trail, 99
Inuit, 31-34, **33**, 43-44, 58, 64, 66,
    77, 80, 82, 83, 85, 88, 107, 111
Inuit Broadcasting Corporation,
    92
Inuit Tapirisat of Canada, 63

inukshuks, 33, **90**, 91
Inuvialuit, 32, 33, 67, 80
Inuvialuit Communications
   Society, 92
Inuvialuit Regional Corporation,
   64
Inuvik, **16**, 35, 62, 94, 104, **105**, 111
Ipellie, Alootook, 88
Iqaluit, 35, 108, **109**, 111
John Paul II, 102
Johnson, Albert, 48
Kalvak, Helen, 120
Keewatin, 62, 106-8, 111
Kenojuak, **78**, 120, **121**
Kitikmeot, 62, 111
Kuptana, Rosemary, 120
Kusugak, Michael, 88
Lake Harbour, **109**
lakes, 15, 75, 112
land claims, 50, 59, 62-63
languages, 29, 44, 111
Larsen, Henry, 39, 121
legislative assembly, **60**, 62, 65, 99,
   114
Liard Highway, **53**
Liard River, 102, 112
libraries, 94
Lindberg Landing, 76
literature, 87-88
Lost Patrol, 48
Lupin mine, **70**, 70-71
McCauley, Cece, 121, **121**
Mackenzie, Alexander, 34, **40**, 41
Mackenzie Highway, 100
Mackenzie Mountains, 11-12, **96**
Mackenzie River, 13-14, 102
Mackenzie River Delta, 13-14, **14**,
   18, 72, 73
McMahon, Pat, 121
magazines, 93
Mandeville Family, 82
maps of Canada,
   political, 123
   topographical, 123
maps of NWT,
   growing season, 125
   political, 124
   precipitation, 125
   principal products, 125
Marble Island, 43, **107**, 108
Markoosie, 88, 121

Matonabbee, 37, 41
May, Wop, **48**, 51
Métis, 34-35, 67, 79-80, 81, 88, 111
Métis Association, 63
mining, 49, 52, 68-71, 114
missionaries, 44-45, 47-48
municipalities, 62-63, 103, 114
museums, 89
music, 87
M.V. Arctic, **68**, 71
Nahanni National Park, **101**, 102
Nahanni River, 10, 12, 102
Nahendeh, 66-67
names for NWT, 9, 66, 111
Native development corporations,
   59
Native Theatre Group, 83
Nerysoo, Richard, 121, **121**
New Western Territory, 66-67
newspapers, 93
non-Native population, 35, 66-67,
   111
Norman Wells, 35, 52, 72, 72-73,
   103
Norris, Dan, 62, 121, **121**
North Pole, 19, 39
North Warning System, 55, **56**
North West Company, 40-41
Northern Arts and Cultural
   Centre, 83
Northern Frontier, 98-99
northern lights, **21**
Northern Traditional Games, 85,
   86, 87
North-West Mounted Police, 47,
   48
Northwest Passage, 37, 38, 39,
   105-6
Northwest Rebellion, 35
NorthwesTel, 95
Nunasi, 73
Nunavut, 9, 64, 66, 67, 98
Nunassiaq, 9
oil and gas, 12, 26, 49, 52, 72-73,
   115
Okheena, Mary, **77**
Oonark, Jessie, **80**, 121
Panagoniak, Charlie, 82
Pangnirtung, 81, 108
Parker, John, 62, 121
parks, 10, 24, 100, 101-2, 108, 114

Parliament, members of, 62
Peary, Robert, 39, 40
Peck, Edmund, 44
performing arts, 82-83
permafrost, 16, 26
Petitot, Émile, 44, 103, 121
Pin, Gino, 99
Pine Point, 52, 53
pingos, 10, **17**, 104
Piqtoukun, David, 122
Pitseolak Ashoona, 121, **122**
Pitseolak, Peter, 121
place names, 37
plant life, 22-23, 26-27, 113
polar bears, 75
Polaris mine, **68**, 71
poljes, **11**
pollution, 27
polygons, **17**
Pond Inlet, 56
population, 28-35, 66-67, 111
Port Radium, 52
postal service, 95
prairie, 12
Precambrian Shield, 10-11
Prince of Wales Northern Heritage
   Centre, 89
radio, 52, 91, 94-95
railways, 53
Ram Plateau, 11, 12, **101**, 102
Ramparts, **103**
Rankin Inlet, 52, 75, 107
recreation, 75, 84-87
Resolute Bay, 56, 109
rivers, 10, 13-14, 112
roads, **46**, 52-53
Royal Canadian Mounted Police,
   39, 47, 48
Ruben, Bertha, 86, 122, **122**
Ruben, Billy, 122
Ryan, Terry, 122
Sahtu, 102-3
St. Roch, **39**
sealing, 73-74
Semmler, Agnes, 122
Sissons, Jack, 89, 122
Slave River, 13, 100
snow geese, 24, 107
soapstone carvings, **58**, 81
social problems, 43-44, 56, 57, 65-66
Spence Bay, 81, 105

Sperry, John R., 122, **122**
sports, 74, 75, 85-86
storytelling, 82
Stringer, Isaac, 122
sunrise and sunset, 19
syllabics, 44
taiga, 22
Taloyoak, 81, 105, 106
Tassoer, Lorna, 82
telephones, 94-95
television, 92-93
Television Northern Canada, 93
Thelon River, 10, 14, 112
Thrasher, Mona, 122
throat singing, 82

Thule people, 32, 108
tourism, 14, 74, 75, 96-109, 115
transportation, 31, 41, 51-53, 71
trapping, 43, 69, 73
treaties, 49-51
Treaty Days, 50
tree line, 19-20, 113
tree species, 22, 113
Trindell, Ted, 88
Trout Lake, **63**, 76
Tsetso, John, 88, 122
Tuktoyaktuk, 53, 77, 104
tundra, **17**, 20, 23, **27**, 33, 113
Tungavik Federation of
    Nunavut, 64

Tunooniq Theatre, 82-83
utilidors, **16**, 17
Viking explorers, 37
Wah-shee, James, 122, **122**
Warner, Glenn, 122
waterfalls, 10, 100
waterways, 13-15, 52, 112
whaling, 33, **42**, 42-43, 108
whooping crane, 24, 25
wild flowers, 22, **23**, 113
Winter Regional Games, 85
Wood Buffalo National Park, 24,
    100
Yellowknife, 5, 35, 52, 61, 62, 63,
    98-99, 111

About the Author

Lyn Hancock, M.A., B.Ed., L.R.A.M., is an award-winning writer, photographer, lecturer, teacher, and the author of a dozen books (including the best-selling *There's a Seal in My Sleeping Bag)* and countless articles on the Northwest Territories. She was born and educated in Australia but has lived in Canada since 1962. Known in the north as the Girl in the Yellow Hat, she has lived and travelled widely in NWT and Yukon since 1972. Currently, she lives in the bush near Fort Simpson.

Picture acknowledgments

Abbreviations for location on page are alone or in combination: T=Top, M=Middle, B=Bottom, L=left, R=Right, I=Inset, BG=Background. All pictures not credited below are the work of the author, Lyn Hancock, © **Franklyn Enterprises**.

Front cover, Menno Fieguth/**Ivy Photo;** 2-3, 25BL,96, 98,106B, © **Brian S. Sytnyk**; 4, 109L, Mike Beedell/**Department of Economic Development & Tourism (ED&T)**; 10R, J. Edwards/**Focus Stock Photo**; 14, 74TL, 103T, © **Paul Von Baich**; 16L, 45L, 56IB, George Peck/**Ivy Photo**; 17L, 33TL, 65IR, 74TR, 90,107B, Dan Heringa/**ED&T**; 17R, 72, **Mia & Klaus**; 20L, 30TL, 87L, **ED&T**; 21, Pat & Rosemarie Keough/**ED&T**; 23I (all),100TR, Wolfgang Weber/**ED&T**; 25TL, 100BR, **Wood Buffalo National Park**; 28TR, Fran Hurcomb/**ED&T**; 28RMB, 42I, 65IL, Doug Walker/**ED&T**; 28BR, 107TL, Lyn Hancock/**ED&T**; 28RMT, 60, 77L, 83BL, 84R, 86L, 118T, 119B, 120MT, 121T, 121B, Tessa Macintosh/**Government NWT (GNWT)**; 36 (C110045), 40IR (C118263), **National Archives of Canada (NAC)**; 38, 40B, 48B, 50T, 51, **Prince of Wales Heritage Centre**; 39, 48T, **RCMP Archives**; 40IL (P-167), **Hudson's Bay Company Archives, Provincial Archives of Manitoba**; 42, Frederick Valiant Cotton/**Hudson's Bay Company Archives, Provincial Archives of Manitoba**; 46, Richard Hartmier/**ED&T**; 68, courtesy **Canarctic Shipping Ltd**; 70 (both) courtesy **Echo Bay Mines Ltd.**; 78, by permission of the **West Baffin Eskimo Cooperative**/courtesy the **Art Gallery of Ontario**; 80L, courtesy of the **estate of Jesse Oonark** and the **National Arts Centre**; 81L, **NWT Native Arts and Crafts Society**; 83T, courtesy of the **Northern Arts and Cultural Centre**; 83R, Bruce Sekulich/**GNWT**; 99R, Douglas Walker/**ED&T**; 101I, **Bill Ivy**; 101R, courtesy of **Nahanni Ram Visitors' Association**; 105TR, **Wolfgang Weber**; 118MB, 118B, 119T, 119MT, 120T, 120MB, 120B, 121MB, 122B, **(GNWT)**; 122MB, **News/North**